Edward Singleton Holden

Our Country's Flag and the Flags of Foreign Countries

Edward Singleton Holden

Our Country's Flag and the Flags of Foreign Countries

ISBN/EAN: 9783337236830

Printed in Europe, USA, Canada, Australia, Japan

Cover: Foto ©ninafisch / pixelio.de

More available books at **www.hansebooks.com**

APPLETONS' HOME READING BOOKS

OUR COUNTRY'S FLAG
AND THE FLAGS OF FOREIGN COUNTRIES

BY

EDWARD S. HOLDEN, LL. D.

NEW YORK
D. APPLETON AND COMPANY
1906

INTRODUCTION TO THE HOME READING BOOK SERIES BY THE EDITOR.

The new education takes two important directions—one of these is toward original observation, requiring the pupil to test and verify what is taught him at school by his own experiments. The information that he learns from books or hears from his teacher's lips must be assimilated by incorporating it with his own experience.

The other direction pointed out by the new education is systematic home reading. It forms a part of school extension of all kinds. The so-called "University Extension" that originated at Cambridge and Oxford has as its chief feature the aid of home reading by lectures and round-table discussions, led or conducted by experts who also lay out the course of reading. The Chautauquan movement in this country prescribes a series of excellent books and furnishes for a goodly number of its readers annual courses of lectures. The teachers' reading circles that exist in many States prescribe the books to be read, and publish some analysis, commentary, or catechism to aid the members.

Home reading, it seems, furnishes the essential basis of this great movement to extend education beyond the school and to make self-culture a habit of life.

Looking more carefully at the difference between the two directions of the new education we can see what each accomplishes. There is first an effort to train the original powers of the individual and make him self-active, quick at observation, and free in his thinking. Next, the new education endeavors, by the reading of books and the study of the wisdom of the race, to make the child or youth a participator in the results of experience of all mankind.

These two movements may be made antagonistic by poor teaching. The book knowledge, containing as it does the precious lesson of human experience, may be so taught as to bring with it only dead rules of conduct, only dead scraps of information, and no stimulant to original thinking. Its contents may be memorized without being understood. On the other hand, the self-activity of the child may be stimulated at the expense of his social well-being—his originality may be cultivated at the expense of his rationality. If he is taught persistently to have his own way, to trust only his own senses, to cling to his own opinions heedless of the experience of his fellows, he is preparing for an unsuccessful, misanthropic career, and is likely enough to end his life in a madhouse.

It is admitted that a too exclusive study of the knowledge found in books, the knowledge which is aggregated from the experience and thought of other people, may result in loading the mind of the pupil with material which he can not use to advantage.

Some minds are so full of lumber that there is no space left to set up a workshop. The necessity of uniting both of these directions of intellectual activity in the schools is therefore obvious, but we must not, in this place, fall into the error of supposing that it is the oral instruction in school and the personal influence of the teacher alone that excites the pupil to activity. Book instruction is not always dry and theoretical. The very persons who declaim against the book, and praise in such strong terms the self-activity of the pupil and original research, are mostly persons who have received their practical impulse from reading the writings of educational reformers. Very few persons have received an impulse from personal contact with inspiring teachers compared with the number that have been aroused by reading such books as Herbert Spencer's Treatise on Education, Rousseau's Émile, Pestalozzi's Leonard and Gertrude, Francis W. Parker's Talks about Teaching, G. Stanley Hall's Pedagogical Seminary. Think in this connection, too, of the impulse to observation in natural science produced by such books as those of Hugh Miller, Faraday, Tyndall, Huxley, Agassiz, and Darwin.

The new scientific book is different from the old. The old style book of science gave dead results where the new one gives not only the results, but a minute account of the method employed in reaching those results. An insight into the method employed in discovery trains the reader into a naturalist, an historian, a sociologist. The books of the writers above named have done more to stimulate original research on the part of their readers than all other influences combined.

It is therefore much more a matter of importance to get the right kind of book than to get a living teacher. The book which teaches results, and at the same time gives in an intelligible manner the steps of discovery and the methods employed, is a book which will stimulate the student to repeat the experiments described and get beyond them into fields of original research himself. Every one remembers the published lectures of Faraday on chemistry, which exercised a wide influence in changing the style of books on natural science, causing them to deal with method more than results, and thus train the reader's power of conducting original research. Robinson Crusoe for nearly two hundred years has aroused the spirit of adventure and prompted young men to resort to the border lands of civilization. A library of home reading should contain books that incite to self-activity and arouse the spirit of inquiry. The books should treat of methods of discovery and evolution. All nature is unified by the discovery of the law of evolution. Each and every being in the world is now explained by the process of development to which it belongs. Every fact now throws light on all the others by illustrating the process of growth in which each has its end and aim.

The Home Reading Books are to be classed as follows:

First Division. Natural history, including popular scientific treatises on plants and animals, and also descriptions of geographical localities. The branch of study in the district school course which corresponds to this is geography. Travels and sojourns in distant lands; special writings which treat of this or that animal or plant, or family of animals or plants; anything that relates to organic nature or to meteorology, or descriptive astronomy may be placed in this class.

Second Division. Whatever relates to physics or natural philosophy, to the statics or dynamics of air or water or light or electricity, or to the properties of matter; whatever relates to chemistry, either organic or inorganic—books on these subjects belong to the class that relates to what is inorganic. Even the so-called organic chemistry relates to the analysis of organic bodies into their inorganic compounds.

Third Division. History, biography, and ethnology. Books relating to the lives of individuals; to the social life of the nation; to the collisions of nations in war, as well as to the aid that one nation gives to another through commerce in times of peace; books on ethnology relating to the modes of life of savage or civilized peoples; on primitive manners and customs—books on these subjects belong to the third class, relating particularly to the human will, not merely the individual will but the social will, the will of the tribe or nation; and to this third class belong also books on ethics and morals, and on forms of government and laws, and what is included under the term civics, or the duties of citizenship.

Fourth Division. The fourth class of books includes more especially literature and works that make known the beautiful in such departments as sculpture, painting, architecture and music. Literature and art show human nature in the form of feelings, emotions, and aspirations, and they show how these feelings lead over to deeds and to clear thoughts. This department of books is perhaps more important than any other in our home reading, inasmuch as it teaches a knowledge of human nature and enables us to understand the motives that lead our fellow-men to action.

PLAN FOR USE AS SUPPLEMENTARY READING.

The first work of the child in the school is to learn to recognize in a printed form the words that are familiar to him by ear. These words constitute what is called the colloquial vocabulary. They are words that he has come to know from having heard them used by the members of his family and by his playmates. He uses these words himself with considerable skill, but what he knows by ear he does not yet know by sight. It will require many weeks, many months even, of constant effort at reading the printed page to bring him to the point where the sight of the written word brings up as much to his mind as the sound of the spoken word. But patience and practice will by and by make the printed word far more suggestive than the spoken word, as every scholar may testify.

In order to bring about this familiarity with the

printed word it has been found necessary to re-enforce the reading in the school by supplementary reading at home. Books of the same grade of difficulty with the reader used in school are to be provided for the pupil. They must be so interesting to him that he will read them at home, using his time before and after school, and even his holidays, for this purpose.

But this matter of familiarizing the child with the printed word is only one half of the object aimed at by the supplementary home reading. He should read that which interests him. He should read that which will increase his power in making deeper studies, and what he reads should tend to correct his habits of observation. Step by step he should be initiated into the scientific method. Too many elementary books fail to teach the scientific method because they point out in an unsystematic way only those features of the object which the untutored senses of the pupil would discover at first glance. It is not useful to tell the child to observe a piece of chalk and see that it is white, more or less friable, and that it makes a mark on a fence or a wall. Scientific observation goes immediately behind the facts which lie obvious to a superficial investigation. Above all, it directs attention to such features of the object as relate it to its environment. It directs attention to the features that have a causal influence in making the object what it is and in extending its effects to other objects. Science discovers the reciprocal action of objects one upon another.

After the child has learned how to observe what is essential in one class of objects he is in a measure fitted to observe for himself all objects that resemble this class. After he has learned how to observe the seeds of the milkweed, he is partially prepared to observe the seeds of the dandelion, the burdock, and the thistle. After he has learned how to study the history of his native country, he has acquired some ability to study the history of England and Scotland or France or Germany. In the same way the daily preparation of his reading lesson at school aids him to read a story of Dickens or Walter Scott.

The teacher of a school will know how to obtain a small sum to invest in supplementary reading. In a graded school of four hundred pupils ten books of each number are sufficient, one set of ten books to be loaned the first week to the best pupils in one of the rooms, the next week to the ten pupils next in ability. On Monday afternoon a discussion should be held over the topics of interest to the pupils who have read the book. The pupils who have not yet read the book will become interested, and await anxiously their turn for the loan of the desired volume. Another set of ten books of a higher grade may be used in the same way in a room containing more advanced pupils. The older pupils who have left school, and also the parents, should avail themselves of the opportunity to read the books brought home from school. Thus is begun that continuous education by means of the public library which is not limited to the school period, but lasts through life. W. T. HARRIS.

WASHINGTON, D. C., *Nov. 16, 1896.*

AUTHOR'S PREFACE.

In Part I of this book a history of the national flag of America is given. It is presented first because every American child should, first of all, know how the flag of his country came to be what it is. Some account is also given of the various standards that were set up on the continent of North America by the early discoverers and explorers. From the settlements at Jamestown in Virginia (1607) and at Plymouth in Massachusetts (1620) until the American Revolution (1775), the flag of England was the flag of the colonists. The king's colors flew on forts and ships of war, but the white ensign with the red cross of St. George was the flag of the people.

The protest of the colonists against unjust rule led to the assumption of liberty-flags in every colony. In 1775 a flag was adopted by the colonies to mark their union for securing, by force if necessary, their rights as Englishmen. On the 4th of July, 1776, the Declaration of American Independence proclaimed "that all political connection between us and the State of Great Britain is, and ought to be, totally dissolved," and a year later the Congress adopted the flag of thirteen stripes with its union of thirteen stars—a new constellation—to symbolize the birth of a new nation.

During the whole history of America, therefore, our flag has been the flag of a *country*, not the personal standard of a king or of an emperor. It stands, and it has stood, for us as the symbol of an abstract idea, not as the sign of the power of any ruler. It is, and it has been, a national flag, not a personal standard.

This is by no means the case with the flags of other and of older nations that have gone through a different development and have had a different history. France, for example, is far older than the United States, yet the French people had no national flag until after the revolution of 1789. Before that time its banners represented the power of the king. They were personal standards, not national flags.

The oriflamme of St. Denis was borne before the armies of France because the French king had succeeded to the honors of knight-banneret of the famous Abbey of St. Denis. It represented the national aspirations in a manner; but it chiefly symbolized the belief that the power of God was on the side of the French monarchs. Ever since the Crusades, the banner of St. George has stood for England, not for the power of the English king.

The idea of nationality has not sprung up in the world all at once. In the beginning of things an army or a tribe gathered round a chief, and his personal standard stood for the power of the army, and the army was the state. As the state grew stronger and more complex the chief of the state became—as in the later years of the Roman Republic—merely its leading citizen and soldier; and the emblems of power grew more and more to represent the majesty of the state itself. The color-bearer of the Roman legion advanced the eagle-standard against the enemy in the name of the Republic and of the commanding general.

Mediaeval Europe was under feudal lords in whom, once more, the power of their petty states was concentrated. Their personal standards once more represented the army and the state. The religious banners given by the Church to lords and princes had something of the character of national banners; and the crosses of different colors borne by the Crusaders (white crosses for the English, red for the French, etc.), distinguished soldiers of different nationalities. But even the Crusaders owed their first fealty to the banners of their personal chiefs. Each knight followed the fortunes of his overlord.

It was not until very recent times that the idea was born that each nationality must have its separate flag. The flag of Germany dates from 1871, that of Italy from 1848; China's flag dates from 1872, Japan's from 1859.

The American boy who reads this book must recollect that his flag, like the flag of England, has always been the flag of a people, and that he unconsciously thinks of it as *his* flag in a stricter and more personal sense than if he were a Bavarian or a Prussian lad, whose national flag—the German—is not yet a generation old. There are centuries of devotion to the symbols of the flag in our English blood.

A large part of this book is taken up with the history of the flags of foreign nations—that is, with the history of the symbols that stand for the hopes, desires, beliefs, and aspirations of countries other than our own.

A flag is a symbol that stands for all these things just as the cross stands for Christianity. How is it that the symbol of the cross really represents Christianity to our thoughts, not merely to our eyes? How is it that a flag, which is nothing more than a bit of colored cloth to our touch or to our sight, really comes to stand for the idea of our country?

The answers to such questions as these are given in Chapter III of this book, and no boy can read it without gaining new and far-reaching conceptions of the antiquity, the universality, and the power of symbols.

Symbols stand close to man and interpret great ideas to him. They enable his feeble imagination to maintain a grasp on vast abstractions like the idea of religion, or of country. Two bits of stick crossed and held aloft have sustained the fainting heart of many a Christian martyr in the presence of the savage beasts of the arena; and the sight of his country's flag has nerved the arm of many a soldier in extremest stress and trial.

A true and complete history of the flags of the world—of national symbols—would be nothing less than a history of the aspirations of men and nations, and of the institutions that they have devised to obtain the object of their hopes and to preserve intact what they have conquered. Not even a sketch of such a history is attempted here. But it is believed that no American child can read these chapters without understanding somewhat of these great matters; nor without acquiring a larger conception of loyalty, of patriotism, and of duty.

E. S. H.

STOCKBRIDGE, *June 17, 1898.*

TO

MASTER ARNOLD WHITRIDGE.

CONTENTS.

CHAPTER	PAGE
INTRODUCTION TO THE HOME READING BOOK SERIES BY THE EDITOR	vii
AUTHOR'S PREFACE	xv
NOTE FOR THE READERS OF THIS BOOK	xxv

PART I.

THE AMERICAN FLAG.

I.—FLAGS OF ENGLAND AND THE AMERICAN COLONIES, 1607–1766	1
FLAGS OF THE AMERICAN COLONIES, 1766–1776	19
II.—THE FLAG OF THE UNITED STATES OF AMERICA, 1777–1795	28
THE FLAG OF THE UNITED STATES OF AMERICA, 1795–1818	34
THE FLAG OF THE UNITED STATES OF AMERICA, 1818–1898	35
OFFICIAL FLAGS	40
THE GREAT SEAL OF THE UNITED STATES OF AMERICA	44

CHAPTER	PAGE
NATIONAL SONGS OF AMERICA	47
THE MEANING OF THE AMERICAN FLAG	56
THE MAN WITHOUT A COUNTRY	62

PART II.

THE FLAGS OF FOREIGN NATIONS.

III.—ANCIENT STANDARDS AND BANNERS—EMBLEMS—SYMBOLS—THE CROSS—ANCIENT FLAGS	65
IV.—THE FLAGS OF FOREIGN NATIONS—ENGLAND—SIGNALING BY FLAGS—UNITED STATES WEATHER BUREAU SIGNALS—SALUTES—FRANCE	91
V.—THE FLAGS OF FOREIGN NATIONS—THE FLAGS OF SOVEREIGN STATES (the different countries are arranged alphabetically for convenient reference)	139

NOTE FOR THE READERS OF THIS BOOK.

It has seemed best to divide this little book into two parts: *First*, the history of the American flag; *second*, some account of flags in general, and of the flags of European nations in particular. The history of the American flag is printed first, because every American child should know that history first of all. Afterward he can read the second part of the book, which will tell him many interesting things about the meaning of flags, and about their uses on land and sea. Many of the excellent plates are printed in colors, but not all of them. A number of those in black and white are drawn so that they also express the colors in the following way:

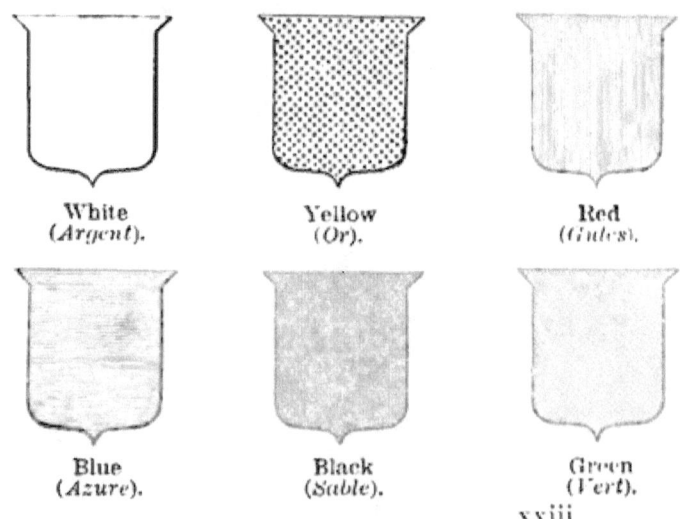

White (*Argent*). Yellow (*Or*). Red (*Gules*).

Blue (*Azure*). Black (*Sable*). Green (*Vert*).

Whenever a surface is left unshaded it stands for white (the French word for silver is *argent*). When the surface is covered with little dots it stands for yellow (the French word for gold is *or*). When the surface is shaded with vertical straight lines it stands for red (the French word corresponding is *gules*); and so on for the other colors. These French words have become English, and they are to be pronounced exactly as they are spelled, according to English rules. If you wish to understand the colors in one of the black and white drawings of this book you should look for the shadings in the different parts of the banner or flag, and read them by this color alphabet.

OUR COUNTRY'S FLAG,

AND THE

FLAGS OF FOREIGN COUNTRIES.

PART I.
THE AMERICAN FLAG.

CHAPTER I.

There is little doubt that the adventurous Northmen from Iceland (a province of Denmark) discovered the continent of America long before the first voyage of Columbus. We know but little of their journeys, and we may say, at any rate, that the discoveries of Columbus, in 1492 and later, made America known to the Old World. It chances that the flags displayed

Fig. 1.—The standard of Spain in 1492. The golden castles on the red fields stand for *Castile*; the red lions on white fields stand for *Leon*.

by the Spaniards when Columbus landed on October 12, 1492, have been described by his own son. They were two—the standard of Spain and the banner of the expedition. These were the first European flags, of which we know anything, that were displayed on the continent of North America.

FIG. 2.—The white banner of the first expedition of Columbus. The green cross stands for Christianity (green is the color of hope); the F and Y for Ferdinand and Ysabel, the King and Queen of Spain.

The many expeditions of discovery in the years following Columbus, and during the sixteenth century, brought other flags to our shores—English, Spanish, French, Portuguese, even Venetian. Each discoverer planted the flag of his country, or perhaps the standard of the monarch under whose patronage his voyage was made. French, Spanish, Swedish, and Dutch colonies were planted on our shores. Americans are most interested in the history of the English colonies and in the flags of England and of our own country.

THE FLAG OF ENGLAND.

We are used to think of our country as one of the youngest in the family of nations, and it is so. But our flag is by no means the youngest of national symbols. It was adopted in 1777 in its present form, and has remained essentially unchanged since 1818. Very many of the present flags of the old countries of Europe are much younger than ours. The French flag was established in 1794. The flag of the German Empire dates from 1871. The flag of Italy was adopted in 1848. Spain's flag, in its present form, is not older than 1785; Portugal's no older than 1830. The Russian tricolor is quite modern.

FLAGS OF ENGLAND AND THE AMERICAN COLONIES, 1607-1766.

England claimed for her colonies in North America all the seacoast from Halifax in Nova Scotia to Cape Fear (near Wilmington) in North Carolina, and all the territory westward from this seacoast—that is, as far as the Pacific Ocean. This immense domain was granted to two companies. The "Plymouth Company" controlled the region from Canada to New York. The "London Company" controlled the region from the Potomac to Cape Fear. A broad strip was left between the two territories, so as to avoid any troubles and disputes about boundaries.

The sovereignty over all the territory remained, of course, in the hands of the English king; but the immediate rule was given to these two companies, just as the rule of India was given (in 1600) to the "East India Company," and just as the rule over parts of Africa was given to the "Imperial British East Africa Company" (1888), or to the "British South Africa Company" in our own days.

The companies of "knights, gentlemen, and merchants" in England furnished the money necessary to send colonists out to America, and expected to gain their profits from trade in lumber, fish, etc. The dominion over the colonies remained with the king and Parliament of England, and the flag of the colonies was of course the English flag. A flag is the visible sign and symbol of dominion.

A full history of the flag of England, which was our flag until the War of the Revolution, is given in the second part of this book. For long centuries, certainly since A. D.

1327 (in the time of King Edward III), the flag of England was the cross of St. George, a red cross on a white field. As St. George's

FIG. 3.—The flag of England (St. George's cross) from 1327 onward.

cross was the flag of the English, so St. Andrew's cross was the flag of the Scottish people. The cross of St. Andrew was white on a blue field. The crosses of St. George and of St. Andrew are shown in their true colors in Plate III, where they are combined with the cross of St. Patrick (for Ireland), which is red on a white ground.

King James VI of Scotland succeeded to

the throne of England (as King James I) in 1603, and the two kingdoms of England and Scotland were united at last after centuries of strife and war. The new sovereignty needed a new flag, and in 1606 the flag was made by uniting the crosses of St. George and of St. Andrew in one field. It was called "the king's colors," not the flag of Great Britain.

Fig. 4.—St. Andrew's cross—the flag of Scotland since the time of the Crusades.

England still had its flag (St. George's cross) and Scotland had its flag also (St. Andrew's cross).

When King Charles I was executed in 1649, England became a Commonwealth un-

FIG. 5.—The king's colors, 1606. In a slightly changed form it is still the color of the reigning monarch of England. See Fig. 35 following.

der Oliver Cromwell, the Lord Protector, and changes were made in the flag that we do not need to know about now. In 1660 Charles II (son of Charles I) was restored to the throne, and changes were again made in the flag of Great Britain.* Early in 1707

---

* Great Britain is England and Scotland, and does not include Ireland. Queen Victoria rules over "the United Kingdom of Great Britain and Ireland," and she is Empress of India.

the "union" flag was adopted as in the next drawing. It was a red ensign, with the symbol of the union of England and Scotland in the upper and inner corner. The space occu-

Fig. 6.—The red ensign of Great Britain, adopted in 1707 and used until 1801, when Ireland was admitted into the union. The flag of most British merchant vessels is like this. The war vessels now fly the cross of St. George on a white field with a union in the upper and inner corner, though they used to display this red ensign—"the meteor flag of England." See Plate III, and also Fig. 35, for the present form of these flags.

pied by the union is called a *canton*, a word which you must remember, as it is often used.

The English flags that are shown in the pictures were the official flags of the colonies in America from 1620 to the Revolutionary War in 1776, when it was declared that "these united colonies are, and of right ought to be, free and independent states." The little ship Mayflower (1620) brought its freight of Pilgrims under the cross of St. George, which was then the flag of all *English* ships. The king's colors, with the union, may also have been displayed, though we have no certain knowledge on this point. British ships of war visiting the coasts of America in later years would certainly fly the king's colors, and finally, after 1707, the red ensign with its "union" was the official flag of Great Britain and of all her colonies.

A flag stands for dominion, for government, for power. And the symbols of the flag tell something of the history and of the aspirations of a people. The cross of St. George was the ancient flag of "Merry England." Under it great battles had been fought. All Englishmen were proud of it. Its cross was the symbol of St. George, the patron saint of England.

The Scottish knights who had traveled

the weary way from Edinburgh to the Holy Land in the wars of the Crusades (A. D. 1095-1270) bore St. Andrew's banner. The two crosses were at last united in the "union" of 1606. The red cross of Ireland was added to the union in 1801. A flag has a meaning then. It embodies a history; it stands for an idea; it may express a hope.

If you think carefully about the flag of any nation—what it is, how it came to be—you will see that this banner is something more than a thing made of colored cloths. It is really visible history. It is the great ideas of the nation expressed in symbols, in forms, in colors. The flag stands for the past history of a people, or at least for that part of it of which they are proud. It stands for the truths they believe in; it stands for the principles they profess.

The flag of England symbolizes a history six centuries long filled with stirring events. The flag of the United States stands for the history of English colonists who have founded a nation for themselves. Every human being under either of these flags is free, entitled to the equal protection of the law, possessed of rights, and not dependent on other men for favors.

Most of the American colonists were devoted and loyal subjects of England. They looked to the "old country" with affectionate remembrance. They were fond of their adopted country at the same time, and their new circumstances gave them a taste for freedom. Every year that passed made them more independent.

But a very considerable number of the colonists were by no means friendly to the mother country. They had suffered persecution from the Church of England, and they had emigrated to a distant land to be rid of religious as well as of political constraint. They were ardent Protestants and above all things they hated "Papists,"—Roman Catholics who obeyed a pope. They were determined to obey nothing but their own consciences—to be their own popes.

As early as 1634 there were mutterings in the colony of Massachusetts Bay that the cross of St. George in the English flag was a papistical symbol. It had been given to an English king by a pope, and blessed by a pope, and it seemed to them to be a sign of obedience to Rome. It was "idolatrous," they said. Therefore it ought not to remain.

This seems a strange idea to us now, for we have accepted the cross as the sign of Christianity. Christ died on the cross, and the symbol belongs to the whole world of Christians. But the Puritans did not feel as we do. To them the cross stood for persecutions that they had not forgotten. It represented a power that was still feared and hated. Accordingly some very zealous and daring spirits at Salem, in Massachusetts, cut the cross out of the banner of the soldiery there, so that it might no longer display a "papistical" symbol. It was a religious scruple that inspired the act, not disloyalty to the English king.

But the flag, with its cross, was the symbol of the dominion of England. It was a sign of the power of the state and of the king, and it was treason to affront that power. So that the people in authority in Boston were in a dilemma. They were afraid to approve the act for fear of offending England; and afraid to disapprove it, for fear of offending their own people.

The matter was finally arranged by allowing the king's colors to be displayed over the castle in Boston harbor, because the castle belonged to the king; and by permitting the different military companies throughout the colonies to choose colors for themselves, which they did. The military company of Newburyport, for instance, in 1684, carried a green flag with the cross of St. George on a white *canton* in its upper and inner quarter.

At the very beginning of the history of the English colonies in America the question of what flag to fly was discussed. The English flag seemed to many of the colonists to represent something they disapproved. So far as it stood for the English state, or for the power of the English king, they found no fault with it. So far as the cross was a papist symbol they hated, despised, and feared it; and the colonists had their own way.

They were so distant from England that no notice was taken of their action. Such actions would not have been permitted to Englishmen at home. It was an important matter, however, because it set the colonists to thinking how far they were really independent of the mother country, and whether they might not some day set up a government and a flag of their own.

All kinds of influences were educating the colonists to be independent of England, and to depend only upon themselves. They were forced to defend themselves against hostile Indians, and to maintain a little army They had to provide for their own defense against foreign enemies, too. In the records of the town of Roxbury in 1673 there are "Tidings of the Dutch assaulting New York, which awakened us to put ourselves in a posture of war, to prepare fortifications, and to seek the face of God."

The religious colonists depended on God to be their helper; and in the matter of war they built their own fortifications, bought their own gunpowder, fired it from their own cannon, and did not rely for any aid upon a mother country three thousand miles over sea, that was busy about its own defenses, and chiefly concerned about its own affairs. The exiled colonists had a new country of their own, they were "subject to this commonwealth and the government *here*," as they declared, and they were ready to defend it against all comers.

As early as 1645 the colonies of Plymouth, Massachusetts Bay, and Connecticut, formed a union for defense, and appointed commissioners to conduct their common defense. Miles Standish * was one of the first commissioners from Massachusetts. This league was the seed from which our union of American States has sprung. From 1643 onward, the idea of such a union was more or less familiar. The "Act of perpetual union between the States" (1776) and the adoption of the "Constitution of the United States" (1788) were mere consequences of this early idea fostered, as it was, by all the conditions of life in a country far removed from the mother kingdom.

So the king's colors were hoisted at the king's forts and on his ships. The people in general had little use for flags, but their military companies displayed special flags of their own. In 1649 Charles I was beheaded, and there was no longer a king. The General Court of Massachusetts ordered in 1651 " that the captain shall advance the aforesaid colors of England upon all necessary occa-

---

* The hero of Longfellow's poem, The Courtship of Miles Standish.

sions." The aforesaid colors were the white flag of St. George, that had lately been adopted by the English Parliament. When King Charles II came back in 1660, the king's colors came with him.

In 1652 Massachusetts coined her pine-tree currency, silver coins, stamped with a pine tree, "as an apt symbol of her progressive vigor." The pine tree appears later upon some New England flags, along with the cross of St. George. The cross would stand for England, and the pine tree would express the fact that the colony claimed a right to its own flag, although it was at the same time an English colony.

England, nowadays, permits her greater colonies, such as Canada, Australia, etc., to coin money and to display a flag. But in the days of Charles II this was considered to be a piece of great presumption, and to show that the New England colonies were on the way to become independent—as indeed they were. There is an anecdote that shows what Charles II thought about the matter.

Charles had been saved from capture after the battle of Worcester (1651) by hiding in an oak tree—the royal oak, so called—

and the figure of the pine tree on the shilling was so rudely made that it might be mistaken for an oak. This was fortunate for

Fig. 7.—The pine-tree flag of New England.

the colonists, because the king was in a great rage when some one showed him the pine-tree currency, and when he learned in this way that New England was presuming to coin money of her own. This was an unpardonable assumption of authority.

But when it was suggested that the tree might be the royal oak which had saved the king's life, his anger was appeased, and he said in good-humor, "Well, after all, they are a parcel of honest dogs!" and was willing to listen to requests made in their behalf.

Each of the older colonies had a *seal* that was stamped on legal papers and the like. These seals were afterward used for the coats of arms of the colonies, and they are now used on the flags of some of the States.*

Some of the colonies had mottoes, and one of these mottoes must be mentioned, because it was often used on flags during the early part of the Revolutionary War. It was adopted by many regiments of New England troops. This is the motto of Connecticut. The seal was a number of grapevines; and the Latin motto, *Qui transtulit sustinet*, means that *He who brought us* (the colonists) *over* (the ocean) *will sustain us*. An early motto of Massachusetts (not its present one) was *An appeal to Heaven*. The mottoes of most of the States are younger than these two, and were adopted when they were admitted into the Union.

---

* The seals of the States may be found in Zieber's Heraldry in America, which is in most large public libraries, and in other books.

FLAGS OF THE AMERICAN COLONIES, 1766–1776.

The flags of England and of her North American colonies have been described in what goes before. The main points to remember are that the flag of England was the red St. George's cross on a white field; that the king's colors were the symbol of the king's power, and the mark of the union of England with Scotland; and that the united New England colonies had a flag of their own.

This last flag was not authorized, nor was it everywhere used; but the people had become accustomed to the idea that New England was in some ways independent of the mother country, and had some right to her own flag. In the southern colonies the flags of England were generally used.

The years from 1766 till the outbreak of the Revolutionary War in 1775, and to the Declaration of Independence in 1776, were troublous times in the colonies. Everywhere the Americans found fault with their British governors, with the laws, and with the taxes laid upon their commerce. It seemed to them that they should have *all* the rights of Englishmen. And one of those rights was not to be taxed unless they had representatives in Parliament to speak for them and to vote upon the matter of taxes.

Many of the laws made in England for the government of the colonies were perfectly just, but a number of them were unreasonable. The royal governors enforced, or tried to enforce, all the laws, just and unjust alike. And the colonists, who began by protesting against the unjust laws, finally came to throwing off their obedience to all laws that they had not themselves made. As early as 1773 it was publicly asked "whether the only asylum for our liberties is not an American commonwealth?" Your school history will have made you familiar with these disputes.

England laid taxes by the "stamp act" of 1765, and this raised such a storm of protests that it was soon repealed. Liberty poles, with flags on them, were set up in protest by the colonists everywhere. The motto on one New Hampshire flag was *Liberty, property, and no stamps*. A New York flag bore the word *Liberty*. In South Carolina, in 1765, the stamped paper was captured and destroyed by the colonists, who hoisted a flag of their own—a blue flag, with three silver crescent moons.

Boston selected a "liberty tree," under which the "sons of liberty" held meetings in 1765. A flag at Taunton bore the words *Liberty and union;* one displayed (1775) in South Carolina the words *Liberty or death.* "Liberty" became a watchword throughout all the colonies. People traveling through New England carried passports from the "sons of liberty" in their own towns to show that they were good Americans.

The aspirations and the hopes of the Americans were then expressed by this one word—*liberty.* They demanded liberty from England. They were convinced that they had a just cause, and that Heaven would help them. A favorite motto on their flags at the beginning of the war of the Revolution was *An appeal to Heaven.* The first Connecticut State troops that fought in the Revolution carried a flag with the State arms and motto *Qui transtulit sustinet.**

No one knows what flags were carried by "the embattled farmers" who fired "the

---

* He who brought us over (the ocean) will sustain us (still), is the meaning of this motto, as has already been said.

shot heard round the world," at Concord,* or at Bunker Hill, though it is said that a pine-tree flag was used at the battle of Bunker Hill.

General Putnam took command of his troops in Cambridge on July 18, 1775, and unfurled a scarlet flag bearing two mottoes, one the motto of Connecticut, *Qui transtulit sustinet*, the other the favorite phrase, *An appeal to Heaven*. In 1776 Massachusetts formally adopted a white flag bearing this last motto, and a green pine tree, as the flag of her naval ships.

The rattlesnake, as a national emblem, was borne on several flags, sometimes with the motto *Don't tread on me*. An emblem of this sort is full of a certain kind of defiant spirit, and it expressed a part of the feeling of the colonists. But it entirely failed to express their conviction that they were striving for liberty; that their appeal to Heaven would be heard; that all the colonies were

---

* This is the first stanza of Emerson's Concord Hymn:

> By the rude bridge that arched the flood,
>   Their flag to April's breeze unfurled,
> Here once the embattled farmers stood,
>   And fired the shot heard 'round the world.

united in a just cause; and, therefore, rattlesnake flags were soon abandoned.

In 1775 and 1776 flags were used bearing stripes—red and blue, or red and white, or white and yellow, or yellow and green. These were usually thirteen in number, to stand for the thirteen colonies in rebellion. The idea of expressing the union of the different colonies by stripes in a flag became familiar to every one very early in the history of the Revolutionary War.

The army under General Washington that besieged the British troops in Boston (July, 1775) was composed of troops from several States, and each company of soldiery had its own flags. Sometimes these were the special standards of the company. Sometimes the State arms were displayed. The Continental Congress was in session in Philadelphia, and it represented "the United Colonies of North America." The troops from the various States were no longer to be State troops, but the army of the colonies; and it was necessary to provide them with a flag that should belong to the "united" colonies, and not to any separate States.

The Continental Congress began to fit

out a navy in October, 1775, and a flag was also needed for its vessels to fly on the high seas. An armed vessel without an authorized flag is everywhere considered to be a pirate. It was clearly necessary to

FIG. 8.—The flag of the United Colonies of America, first displayed in General Washington's camp, January 2, 1776.

adopt a flag for the navy and for the Continental army as well, and the Congress appointed a committee, with Dr. Benjamin Franklin at its head, to go to Cambridge, to consult with General Washington, and to recommend such a flag.

The new flag was first displayed at the camp before Boston in January, 1776, and it represented the exact situation of affairs. If we understand just how men felt at this time, we shall see that the flag adopted expressed the general feeling precisely.

If one of us now thinks of that camp before Boston, commanded by General Washington, whose soldiers were besieging the British regulars, a hundred years ago, it seems for a moment that the strife was between Americans and foreigners. Here was an army of foreigners holding Boston, and an army of Americans besieging them, and the motto of the Americans was *Liberty*. And by *liberty* we now understand complete independence from British rule.

But this was not the idea of the colonists. *Liberty* to them meant freedom from oppressive English laws. They were fighting for the freedom that other Englishmen enjoyed. They called themselves Englishmen —Englishmen living in America. No one thought of the British troops as foreigners.* We were rebellious English colonists, united together to resist unjust taxation, not Americans banded against a foreign foe. It was

---

* Not until Hessian and other German troops were hired by England to fight in America.

not until the Declaration of Independence (July 4, 1776) that the colonists entirely threw off their allegiance to England.

The flag displayed over Washington's camp at Cambridge in January of that year exactly expressed the general situation. The thirteen stripes symbolized the thirteen colonies—

New Hampshire,
Massachusetts,
Rhode Island,
Connecticut,
New York,
New Jersey,
Pennsylvania,
Delaware,
Maryland,
Virginia,
North Carolina,
South Carolina,
Georgia.

The "union" in the *canton* was the king's colors. The colonies acknowledged their allegiance to England and to the king, only they wanted justice; they wanted their rights as Englishmen; and they were united in a determination to secure these rights, and to fight for them if fighting was necessary. General Washington says of this flag: "We hoisted the Union flag in compliment to the united colonies, and saluted it with thirteen guns."

The same flag, probably, was hoisted on the naval ship of John Paul Jones at about the same time. It is said that this very same flag was one of the signal flags of the British navy before the days of the Revolution, and that it was the sign for the "red" division of a fleet to give battle. However this may be, it is not at all likely that such an English signal flag had ever been displayed in American waters; and it is practically certain that the English signal had nothing whatever to do in suggesting the flag hoisted over General Washington's army in 1776.

CHAPTER II.

THE FLAG OF THE UNITED STATES OF AMERICA, 1777–1898.

On the 2d of July, 1776, the American Congress resolved "that these united colonies are, and of right ought to be, free and independent States; and that all political connection between us and the state of Great Britain is, and ought to be, totally dissolved." On the 4th of July a declaration of independence was adopted by the Congress, and sent out under its authority, to announce to all other nations that the United States of America claimed a place among them. On this 4th of July the nation was born. Its flag, the visible symbol of its power, was not adopted till 1777.

On the 14th of June, 1777, Congress resolved "that the flag of the thirteen United States be thirteen stripes, alternate red and white; that the union be thirteen stars, white in a blue field, representing a new constellation."

The national flag—*our* national flag—grew in the most direct way out of the banners that had waved over the colonists. The

FIG. 9.—The flag of the United States of America, 1777–1795.

flag of the United *Colonies* had thirteen stripes, one for each colony, and the stripes were alternate red and white. This part of the old flag remained unchanged in the new one. Each colony retained its stripe.

The flag of the colonies, in its union, had displayed the king's colors. There was now no longer a king in America, but a new Union had arisen—a Union of thirteen States—no longer a Union of kingdoms. The union of the old flag had been the crosses of St. George and St. Andrew conjoined on a blue field. The new union was a circle of silver stars in a blue sky—"a new constellation."

The flag of the United States was derived from the flag of the United Colonies in the simplest and most natural manner. The old flag had expressed the hopes and aspirations of thirteen colonies which had united in order to secure justice from their king and fellow-countrymen in England. The new flag expressed the determined resolve of the same thirteen colonies—now become sovereign States—to form a permanent Union, and to take their place among the nations of the world. They were no longer Englishmen: they were Americans.

Many suggestions have been made to account for the appearance of stars or of stripes in the new flag. It seems unnecessary to seek for any explanation other than the one that has just been given. The old flag of the United Colonies expressed the feelings and aspirations of the revolted English colonists. They were willing to remain as subjects of the English king, but they had united to secure justice. The new flag expressed their firm resolve to throw off the yoke of England, and to become a new nation. The symbols of each flag exactly expressed the feeling of the men who bore it.

There is a resemblance between the colors and symbols of the new flag and the symbols borne on the coat of arms of General Washington that is worthy of remark. General Washington was a descendant of an English family, and his ancestors bore a coat of arms that he himself used as a seal, and for a bookplate.

It has been supposed that the stars of the American flag were suggested by the three stars of this coat of arms, and this is not impossible. General Washington was in Philadelphia in June, 1777, and he is said to have engaged Mrs. John Ross, at that time, to make the first flag, though this is not absolutely certain.

However this may be, it is known that the American flag of thirteen stars and of thirteen stripes was displayed at the siege of Fort Stanwix in August, 1777; at the battle of Brandywine on September 11th; at Germantown on the 4th of October; at the surrender of the British under General Burgoyne on October 17th. The flag had been adopted

FIG. 10.—The coat of arms (bookplate) of General George Washington. The field of the shield is white (*argent*), the two bars are red (*gules*), as well as the three stars.

in June of the same year. The vessels of the American navy flew this flag on the high seas, and their victories made it respected everywhere.

It is curious to note that so late as 1784 the American flag was not always represented correctly in drawings made by foreigners. In a German publication of that year* the union is made to cover the upper *six* stripes only (instead of seven), though the drawing is otherwise accurate. Let the American child who is reading this chapter stop here and try to draw the flag of his country without looking at any of the illustrations. Every one should be able to do this.

The treaty of peace between England and the United States was signed (at Paris, France) on September 3, 1783. This was the acknowledgment by Great Britain of the independence of her former colonies; and the other nations of Europe stood by consenting. Our flag was admitted, at that time, on equal terms with the standards of ancient kingdoms and states, to the company of the banners of the world.

In 1791 Vermont was admitted to the Union, and in 1792 Kentucky became a State. No change was made in the national

---

* Sprengel's Allgemeines Taschenbuch für 1784 in the Lenox Library of New York city.

flag till 1794, when Congress ordered "that from and after the first day of May, 1795, the flag of the United States be fifteen

Fig. 11.—The flag of the United States from 1795 to 1818. The War of 1812 was fought under this flag.

stripes, alternate red and white; and that the union be fifteen stars, white in a blue field."

Tennessee was admitted to the Union in 1796, Ohio in 1802, Louisiana in 1812, Indiana in 1816, Mississippi in 1817, and Illinois in 1818, making twenty States in all. It was plain that the vast territory of the United States would be carved up into other

States from time to time. Accordingly, in April, 1818, the Congress passed

"AN ACT TO ESTABLISH THE FLAG OF THE UNITED STATES.

"SECTION 1. *Be it enacted, etc.*, That from and after the fourth day of July next, the flag of the United States be thirteen horizontal stripes, alternate red and white; that the Union have twenty stars, white in a blue field.

"Section 2. *And be it further enacted*, That on the admission of every new State into the Union, one star be added to the union of the flag; and that such addition shall take effect on the fourth of July next succeeding such admission. *Approved*, April 4, 1818."

No changes (other than the addition of new stars) have been made in the national flag since 1818. The stars have been added, one by one, until in 1898 there are forty-five in all. Every State has its star; each of the original thirteen States has its stripe. The territories are not represented in the flag. Plate I, the frontispiece, represents the national flag on July 4, 1895. Utah has since been admitted, and another star was added on July 4, 1896.

Fig. 12.—The flag of the United States in 1898. It has forty-five stars. More will be added in the future.

So long as the United States exists the flag will remain in its present form, except that new stars will be displayed as the new States come in. It will forever exhibit the origin of the nation from the thirteen colonies, and its growth into a Union of sovereign States.

The field of the flag is already somewhat crowded with its constellation of forty-five stars, and it is not too soon to inquire what is to be done if ten more States are admitted into the Union. Fifty-five stars arranged in rows would confuse the field, and take away the distinctness, and some of the dignity, of the flag. A very simple solution would be to group the stars into one large star. At a distance only one star would show. Near by it would be seen that this one star was made up of many small ones. The only possible objection to this plan is that our flag would then somewhat resemble the ensign of Liberia (which has one star and eleven stripes—see Plate IX); but it appears that this objection is not of much weight.

The frontispiece gives a true representation of the flag both as to colors and as to proportions. Flags are made of wool "bunting." The stars are white, sewed to the blue *canton* on both sides. The "heading" (that part of the flag nearest the staff) is of strong canvas, with two holes, brass-rimmed ("grommets"), for the "halyards" (ropes).

The garrison-flag, 36 by 20 feet, is the official flag at all army posts. The post-flag is 20 by 10 feet, and the storm-flag is 8 feet by 4 feet 2 inches.*

---

* The usual price of a flag 4 feet long is about $1.75; for one 6 feet long about $4.50; for one 12 feet long about $10; for one 20 feet long about $25; for one 40 feet long about $80.

In the opinion of most persons the flag of the United States is used too freely, and with too little respect—for advertising purposes, as a trade-mark, etc. A movement is on foot to regulate its use in such ways, and several of the States are considering laws to restrain its improper display. Such laws should be very carefully drawn so as not to impose restrictions that are merely vexatious. The more the flag is displayed the better, provided that it is always done in a respectful manner.

The flag of the United States was established on June 14, 1777. One of the patriotic hereditary societies of Pennsylvania (the Colonial Dames of America) has made the excellent suggestion that the 14th day of June in every year should hereafter be known as "Flag Day," and that it should be commemorated by the display of the American flag from every home in the land. Flag Day was first observed in 1893. It is too soon to say whether this is to become one of the nation's gala days, but there seems to be every reason why it should be celebrated.

There are special flags for some of the departments at Washington, and for some of the higher officers of the government. For instance, the revenue marine is a branch of the Treasury Department. Its officers are charged with the duty of boarding vessels as they enter our harbors and with the enforcement of the laws of the United States relating to customs duties, etc. The revenue marine has a distinguishing flag for its vessels. The national ensign is also displayed.

The distinguishing flag of the revenue marine is shown in Plate II. The yachts belonging to American citizens have a special flag that gives them certain privileges. The ensign of American yachts at home or abroad is also shown in Plate II. The national ensign, the distinguishing flag of the revenue marine and the yacht flag, may be seen in almost every American port, and they are mentioned here for this reason.

Flags are extensively used in the navy and in the army for signals, and some account of signal flags is given in the second part of this book. (See Plate IV.) Every naval ship has a "code book," by means of which she can convey messages to other ships (if they have the same book). All merchant ships use a mercantile code for a like purpose.

The ships of our navy fly the national ensign, and also the "jack," which is nothing but the union of the flag—a blue field with white stars. It is shown in Plate II. They also fly a personal flag for the commander; he may be the "senior officer present," or a commodore, or a rear admiral, etc. If the Secretary of the Navy, or the President of the United States is on board their personal flags are displayed. The President's flag is also shown in Plate II.

The flags of a ship tell all the other ships of a squadron, or of foreign navies, something about her mission, her commander, her passengers, etc. She has a signal alphabet of flags for use in peace or war. The flags are used by day, and signal lights (blue, white, green, red) by night.

The army, too, has distinguishing flags for its regiments of engineers, artillery, infantry, and cavalry. Each regiment has its own "regimental color" (a blue silk flag for the infantry, a red for the artillery, a yellow for the cavalry, with the American eagle and coat of arms), and also carries a special

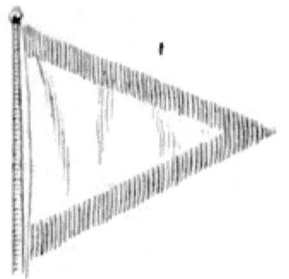
Naval Convoy.

Commodore.

Senior Officer present.

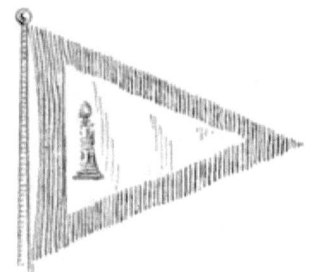
Light-house Service.

Secretary of the Navy.

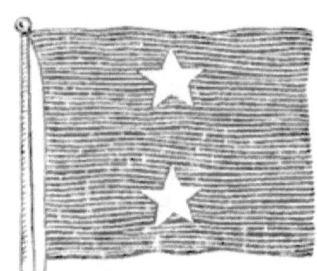
Rear Admiral.

Union Jack.

President of the United States.

FIG. 13.—Some official flags of the United States.

national flag about six feet square. On the stripes are written the names of the battles in which the regiment has taken part.

One of the older regiments displays a proud history in this way. Its flag may bear the names of New Orleans (1815), Buena Vista (1847), and a host of hard-fought battles of the civil war, as well as Santiago or Manila (1898). Regiments are united into brigades (of three or more regiments), brigades into divisions (of three or more brigades), divisions into army corps (of three or more divisions), and each of these bodies has its distinguishing flag. The militia regiments of the various State troops carry the national colors, and they usually carry the flag of their State also.

In both army and navy the greatest respect is paid to the flag. The interior loyalty that every American should feel is expressed by outward signs of respect. In an army camp the colors are brought to the "color line" (a line of stacked rifles in the front of the camp) at guard mounting in the morning, and they are laid on the line of guns. Whoever crosses that line during the day must salute the colors by touching his cap.

At evening parade the colors are brought, under the escort of the "color guard," to their place in the line of battle. The regiment salutes them, the band plays The Star-spangled Banner, and all visitors to the camp are expected to rise and remain standing while the band is playing the national anthem. At all military posts, forts, etc., the flag is hoisted at *reveille*, and remains flying till sunset.

On board of an American ship of war there is a similar etiquette. The flag is hoisted at eight o'clock in the morning with ceremony, and remains flying till sunset. Every one who comes on the quarter deck salutes by touching his cap. It is really a salute to the colors. Merchant vessels salute each other by lowering their flags and then quickly hoisting them again—by "dipping the flag," as it is called. A man-of-war should never lower her flag except to surrender, or as a courtesy to another vessel that has first given a like salute.

A ship in distress hoists its flag with the union *down*. A flag at half mast is a sign of mourning.* A white flag is everywhere recognized as a signal of peace. A yellow flag (a hospital flag) is a sign that wounded men, or the sick, are sheltered by it. A white flag bearing a red cross is the standard of the Geneva Red Cross Association for the relief of the wounded. A black flag is the flag of pirates, and has often been flown by the buccaneers of the Spanish Main, either with or without the skull and cross bones. The red flag has of late years come to be considered the flag of Socialists or of anarchists. The second part of this book gives more particulars about these matters.

THE GREAT SEAL OF THE UNITED STATES.

The design for the flag of the United States was adopted in 1777. On the 4th of July, 1776, a Committee of Congress was appointed "to prepare a device for a seal of the United States of North † America."

---

* The flag should be hoisted at half mast on Decoration Day (May 30th) and kept there until noon, when it should be run to the top of the staff and only lowered at sunset.

† It is to be noted that this word is not a part of the official name of the country, which is the United States of America. If the whole of South America were to join the Union, no change in the name of the country would be necessary. From

THE GREAT SEAL OF THE UNITED STATES.

The seal was not adopted till 1782, however. The reader should look carefully at the illustration. The coins of the United States bear these devices in whole or in part.*

The coat of arms of the United States is that portion of the illustration inside the border. The shield is *argent* (white) six pallets *gules* (red) with an azure "chief." It is borne on the breast of an American eagle, holding in his dexter talon an olive branch with thirteen leaves and fruits (in sign of peace), and in his sinister a sheaf of as many arrows (in menace of war). The eagle, the olive, and the arrows are blazoned in their proper colors.

FIG. 14.—The great seal of the United States of America, adopted in 1782.

the beginning our people have called themselves "Americans," not "North Americans"; and we always speak of our country as "America."

* They are best seen on the reverse side of the twenty-dollar gold piece. Of late years the motto "In God we Trust" has been added to our coins. It is no part of the coat of arms.

Above the eagle's head is an azure sky with silver stars arranged in groups of one, four, three, four, one stars. They are surrounded by a golden halo, and encircled with clouds. In the beak of the eagle is a golden scroll bearing the motto *E pluribus Unum* ("out of many, one"—that is, one Union has been formed out of many States).

There are several points to be noticed in comparing the arms (seal) with the flag. The outer edges of the shield of the coat of arms are argent (white); the outer stripes of the flag are gules (red). The "chief" of the arms, like the "canton" of the flag, is blue; but it does not bear any stars. Thirteen stars are displayed above the head of the eagle in the seal, while the flag bears forty-five stars at present, and will bear other stars in the future. The flag will be changed from time to time. The seal will remain in the future as it was in 1782.

The golden halo round the stars of the seal and the clouds encircling the halo do not appear in the flag, nor does the olive branch, the sheaf of arrows, or the motto. The eagle appears in the flag of the revenue-marine service, but not in the national colors. These small differences are worthy of remark, because every American child should be entirely familiar with the emblems of his own country.*

NATIONAL SONGS OF AMERICA.

Properly speaking, America has no national song. The two poems that follow, The Star-spangled Banner and The American Flag, are the best known among many verses of the kind. The first of them—The Star-spangled Banner—comes nearer to being a really national song than any other. It is regularly played by the bands on our war vessels, and at military posts at evening parade, and is recognized by foreign countries as the nation's anthem.

The country is yet waiting for a thoroughly representative poem that shall express the whole of the nation's aspirations, and that shall be set to original and stirring music. Until we have such verses

---

* Both the seal and the flag of the United States are composed according to the strictest laws of heraldry: a set of rules that governs such matters. Its rules date from the Crusades. The seals of some of the States do not follow any rules at all, and are sadly in need of change.

from an American poet, and such original music from one of our own composers, the Star-spangled Banner will probably stand for our national song.

Its chief lack as a poem is that it describes a single incident only. Its tune was borrowed from a piece of music for the flute (Anacreon in Heaven) and is quite difficult to sing. Not one American in a thousand knows the words of the poem, and the air is not accurately known by most persons. The words of a truly national hymn should be in the memory of every one, and its air should be stirring and easily remembered and sung.

Yankee Doodle—with trivial words and music borrowed from an English tune of the time of Charles II—was a favorite during the War of the American Revolution. The Star-spangled Banner owes its origin to an incident of the War of 1812. The war of the rebellion (1861–65) produced hundreds of war songs, some of them of real excellence. No truly *national* song could arise, of course, out of a civil war, which divided the people among themselves, and set brother at strife with brother.

We are still waiting for a national song that shall be dignified, serious, expressive of the aspirations and of the ideals of the whole people. It must not be boastful; it must not be sanguinary; it must not breathe vengeance. We are a serious-minded and a religious people, devoted to ideals of justice, of equal law, of absolute fair dealing, of charity to our fellow men.

Our national anthem, when it is written, must express the nation's trust in God; its devout confidence in a just cause; its devotion to right; its determination to die rather than to submit to injustice or to wrong. Any trivial boastfulness, any childish delight in the pomp and circumstance of war, any pleasure in vengeance, is unworthy and undignified. The national song of America should breathe the spirit of a Washington and of a Lincoln, not that of a Cæsar or of a Napoleon.

Of late years, some enthusiasts have taken to calling the flag of our country by the name of "Old Glory." There is no question that those who use this name intend to express their affection for the national symbol, and in so far no objection can be made to the epithet. But there is also no doubt that the excessive familiarity and lack of respect in the phrase offends, to some degree, against good taste. It expresses a part, but only a part, of the true feeling of the nation.

There is certainly a shade of boastfulness in the "Glory"; and there is too much triviality and familiarity in the "Old." There is a total lack of dignity in the combination. A flag represents an ideal that is, in its degree, sacred, somewhat as the symbol of the cross is sacred. Respect, reverence, devotion, are called for, such as serious men can give; not the trivial endearments of boon companions or of thoughtless children.

President Lincoln was a true martyr and hero; he became the idol of his countrymen. No doubt some of those who really venerated his virtues and high-mindedness expressed their belief in his wisdom and patriotism by some such phrase as, "Old Lincoln—Old Abe—will rule the country right." There is nothing but praise to give to the spirit that prompted homely words of the sort. Even the form of it might be pardoned so long as the great President was still with us. After he was laid in his martyr's grave who can doubt that a phrase in this form would grate —solely on account of its form—most harshly on the ear? A trivial phrase of homely and affectionate familiarity is no longer adequate. Language at once more respectful, more serious, more dignified, more formal, is demanded.

In the same way our flag, which is, we hope, not for a day but for all time, must not be spoken of as if it were a boon companion, but rather a sacred symbol of great ideals. As we demand for our American ideals the respect that they deserve, so we should exact the forms of respect for the flag that represents them. The flag is not the familiar possession of any man or of any company of men. It is the symbol of the whole nation and it represents its long history in the past and the totality of its aspirations for the future. It should receive from each one of us every kind of respect; the respect of dignified and measured phrase as well as the interior reverence which can only find its fit expression in this way.

THE STAR-SPANGLED BANNER.

By Francis Scott Key.*

I.

Oh! say, can you see by the dawn's early light
  What so proudly we hailed at the twilight's last
    gleaming,
Whose broad stripes and bright stars through the
    perilous fight,
  O'er the ramparts we watched, were so gallantly
    streaming?
And the rockets' red glare, the bombs bursting in
    air,
Gave proof through the night that our flag was still
    there.
Oh! say, does the star-spangled banner yet wave
O'er the land of the free and the home of the brave?

---

* Francis Scott Key, the poet, was born in Maryland in 1779, and died in 1843. During the war of 1812–15 between the United States and Great Britain the English fleet bombarded Fort McHenry, near Baltimore, on September 13, 1814. During the whole of that day and night he witnessed the British bombardment of the fort; and on the following morning he and his American friends saw with delight that the fort was still ours; and that the American flag, torn with shot and shell, was still waving in its place. The story is told in the poem. The flag that flew at Fort McHenry still exists, and was exhibited at the Centennial Exhibition in Philadelphia in 1876 full of rents made by the enemy's cannonade. A statue to Francis Scott Key stands in Golden Gate Park in San Francisco.

II.

On the shore, dimly seen through the mists of the deep,
  Where the foe's haughty host in dread silence reposes;
What is that which the breeze, o'er the towering steep,
  As it fitfully blows, half conceals, half discloses?
Now it catches the gleam of the morning's first beam,
In full glory reflected now shines in the stream—
'Tis the star-spangled banner; oh! long may it wave
O'er the land of the free and the home of the brave.

III.

And where is that band who so vauntingly swore
  That the havoc of war and the battle's confusion,
A home and a country should leave us no more?
  Their blood has washed out their foul footsteps' pollution.
No refuge could save the hireling and slave
From the terror of flight, or the gloom of the grave,
And the star-spangled banner in triumph doth wave
O'er the land of the free and the home of the brave.

IV.

Oh! thus be it ever when freemen shall stand
  Between their loved homes and the war's desolation;
Blest with victory and peace, may the Heav'n-rescued land
  Praise the Power that hath made and preserved us a nation.

Then conquer we must when our cause it is just,
And this be our motto, "In God is our Trust."
And the star-spangled banner in triumph shall wave
O'er the land of the free and the home of the brave.

THE AMERICAN FLAG.

By Joseph Rodman Drake.*

I.

When Freedom from her mountain height,
   Unfurled her standard to the air,
She tore the azure robe of night,
   And set the stars of glory there.
She mingled with its gorgeous dyes
The milky baldric † of the skies,
And striped its pure, celestial white
With streakings of the morning's light;
Then from her mansion in the sun
She called her eagle-bearer down,
And gave into his mighty hand
The symbol of her chosen land.

II.

Majestic monarch of the cloud!
   Who rear'st aloft thy eagle form
To hear the tempest trumpings loud,
And see the lightning lances driven,

---

* Joseph Rodman Drake, the poet, was born in New York in 1795, and died in 1820. The poem was written in 1819.

† Baldric = a shoulder belt for a sword.

When stride the warriors of the storm,
And rolls the thunder-drum of Heaven!
Child of the Sun!* to thee 'tis given
   To guard the banner of the free!
To hover in the sulphur smoke,
To ward away the battle stroke,
And bid its blendings shine afar,
Like rainbows on the cloud of war,
   The harbingers † of victory.

III.

Flag of the brave! thy folds shall fly
The sign of hope and triumph high;
When speaks the trumpet's signal tone,
And the long line ‡ comes gleaming on,
Ere yet the life-blood, warm and wet,
Has dimmed the glistening bayonet,
Each soldier's eye shall brightly turn
To where thy sky-born glories burn;
And, as his springy steps advance,
Catch war and vengeance from the glance;
And when the cannon-mouthings loud
Heave in wild wreaths the battle shroud,
And gory sabers rise and fall,
Like shoots of flame on midnight's pall—
Then shall thy meteor glances glow,
   And cowering foes shall sink beneath
Each gallant arm that strikes below
   That lovely messenger of death!

---

  * Child of the Sun = the eagle, that can gaze upon the sun without averting its eyes.

  † Harbingers = forerunners; heralds.

  ‡ The long advancing line of soldiers.

IV.

Flag of the seas! on Ocean's wave
Thy stars shall glitter o'er the brave;
When death, careering on the gale,
Sweeps darkly round the bellied sail,
And frighted waves rush wildly back,
Before the broadside's reeling rack,*
Each dying wanderer of the sea
Shall look at once to Heaven and thee,
And smile to see thy splendors fly
In triumph o'er his closing eye.

V.

Flag of the free heart's hope and home!
  By angel's hands to valor given;
Thy stars have lit the welkin † dome,
  And all thy hues were born in Heaven.
Forever float that standard sheet!
  Where breathes the foe but falls before us,
With Freedom's soil beneath our feet,
  And Freedom's banner streaming o'er us.

THE MEANING OF THE AMERICAN FLAG.

Many eloquent speeches have been made that recite what the flag should stand for to a citizen of America. Among them two are here selected:

---

* The waves rush back affrighted before the smoke of the cannon of the broadside guns.

† The welkin = the hollow vault of the sky.

"As at the early dawn the stars shine forth even while it grows light, and then, as the sun advances, that light breaks into banks and streaming lines of color, the glowing red and intense white striving together and ribbing the horizon with bars effulgent; so, on the American flag, stars and beams of many colored light shine out together....

"It is the banner of dawn. It means *Liberty;* and the galley slave, the poor oppressed conscript, the down-trodden creature of foreign despotism, sees in the American flag that very promise and production of God: 'The people which sat in darkness, saw a great light; and to them which sat in the region and shadow of death, light is sprung up.'

"In 1777, within a few days of one year after the Declaration of Independence, the congress of the colonies in the confederated states assembled and ordained this glorious national flag which we now hold and defend, and advanced it full high before God and all men as the flag of liberty. It was no holiday flag gorgeously emblazoned for gayety or vanity. It was a solemn national symbol....

"Our flag carries American ideas, American history, and American feelings. Beginning with the colonies, and coming down to our time, in its sacred heraldry, in its glorious insignia, it has gathered and stored chiefly this supreme idea: *Divine right of liberty in man.* Every color means liberty; every thread means liberty; every form of star and beam or stripe of light means liberty; not lawlessness, not license; but organized, institutional liberty—liberty through law, and laws for liberty!

"It is not a painted rag. It is a whole national history. It is the Constitution. It is the Government. It is the free people that stand in the government on the Constitution." —From the address of the Rev. Henry Ward Beecher to members of the Fourteenth Regiment of New York State Troops in 1861.

"There is the national flag! He must be cold indeed who can look upon its folds rippling in the breeze without pride of country. If he be in a foreign land, the flag is companionship, and the country itself, with all its endearments. Who, as he sees it can think of a State merely? Whose eye, once fastened upon its radiant trophies can fail to

recognize the image of the whole nation?...
Its highest beauty is in what it symbolizes.
It is because it represents all that all gaze
upon it with delight and reverence....

"Its stripes of alternate red and white
proclaim the original union of thirteen States
to maintain the Declaration of Independence.
Its stars, white on a field of blue, proclaim
that union of States constituting our national
constellation which receives a new star with
every new State. The two together signify
union, past and present. The very colors
have a language.... White is for purity;
red for valor; blue for justice; and all together—bunting, stripes, stars and colors,
blazing in the sky—make the flag of our
country, to be cherished by all our hearts, to
be upheld by all our hands."—Charles Sumner, Senator from Massachusetts.

The speeches of Sumner and of Beecher
show the meanings that eloquent and patriotic
civilians find in the flag. Soldiers show their
devotion to it in more direct and immediate
ways. Out of a thousand incidents that
might be quoted from the history of the wars
of the United States, one is here set down.
It exhibits the passionate devotion of loyal

soldiers to the standard under which they serve, which is to them the symbol of the cause and the country that they give their lives to defend.

In the year 1863 the Sixteenth Regiment of Connecticut volunteers, after three days' hard fighting, was forced to surrender with the rest of the command. Just before the enemy swarmed over the breastworks that they had defended for so long, the colonel of the regiment shouted to his men to save the colors—not to let the flag fall into the hands of the enemy. In an instant the battle flags were stripped from their poles and cut and torn into small fragments. Every piece was carefully hidden in the best way possible.

The regiment, some five hundred strong, was sent to a prison camp where most of the men remained until the close of the war. Each piece of the colors was sacredly preserved. When a soldier died his piece was intrusted to a comrade. At the end of the war the weary prisoners returned to their homes, each bringing his bit of star or stripe with him. All these worn fragments were patched together and the regimental colors, nearly complete, are now preserved in the State House at Hartford.

No devotion could be more simple, more resolute, more absolute, than this. And their love of the flag was not shown alone by their willingness to die for it on the field of action. They lived for it through long years of imprisonment, and brought it back whole to the State that gave it into their hands to honor and defend.

The adventurous sailors of the United States have displayed the flag in every part of the world where commerce called them, from the Arctic to the Indies. Our navy has made it respected in peace and in war. It has been planted in foreign countries by armed force, in Tripoli (1805), in Mexico (1846), in Manila, Porto Rico, and Cuba (1898).

The exploring expedition of Commodore Wilkes carried it through the Pacific Ocean and to the Antarctic regions (1839). The Arctic expeditions of Kane (1850–53), Hayes (1860), Hall (1871), De Long (1879), Greely (1881–'83), Peary (1891–98) have unfurled the flag among the icebergs of the extremest North. Stanley has carried it to the heart of

Africa (1871 and later). It is respected everywhere, and everywhere it stands for American freedom, energy, vigor.

THE MAN WITHOUT A COUNTRY.

Every American child ought to read a little book written in 1863, during the war of the Rebellion, by the Rev. Edward Everett Hale, called The Man without a Country. This masterpiece recites the story of a young officer of the army, Philip Nolan by name, who had joined in Aaron Burr's plot to overthrow the Government of the United States in 1805. When Nolan was tried by a military court he exclaimed, in a moment of passion, that he wished he might never hear the name of the United States again.

The sentence of the court on Nolan, who was misguided and not willfully a traitor, was that his wish should be carried out, and that he should, in fact, never hear the name of his country spoken, nor know anything of her history so long as he should live.

According to the story, Nolan spent a long life, always at sea on some one of the naval vessels of the country, always in company with the officers of the fleet, always well treated and even loved by his companions; but never hearing the name of his country spoken, never allowed to see a book or a newspaper that told of her prosperity, never permitted to converse with any stranger who might tell him of her progress and of her glory. He lived a long life, always a man without a country, knowing nothing of home or friends.

At last, when he came to die, the flag was brought to him, and one of his faithful companions told him the story of each star in the Union, star by star. The whole of her glorious history was unfolded amid the old man's tears. During all the long years of his life he had thought of this history, guessed it out bit by bit, and had loved his country as none but an exile can. His heart had been changed long before, but he had submitted to his just punishment with manly resignation. His whole life had been an expiation for the folly and mistake of his rash youth.

This pitiful tale is not true. It is a mere piece of imagination. But it pictures the misery and suffering of a man who has willfully separated himself from his comrades and who has cut himself off from all the benefits and joys of association with his fellow men. It teaches, as no other writing can, the meaning of patriotism, and the signification of a flag.

PART II.
THE FLAGS OF FOREIGN NATIONS.

CHAPTER III.

ANCIENT STANDARDS AND BANNERS—EMBLEMS—SYMBOLS—THE CROSS—ANCIENT FLAGS.

The very earliest standards were the symbols of the power of a king or of his military commanders. The god Hercules was the standard of Alexander the Great. A city, like Athens, had an emblem of its own. The owl of Athens stood for the power of the city. Such emblems were often of religious origin, and had a sacred significance. The Egyptians, for instance, bore sacred emblems on their military standards, and these emblems were devised by the priests. Sometimes they carried a tablet inscribed with the king's name.

The ancient Hebrews had standards for the various tribes. The Old Testament recites (Numbers i, 52) that every man pitched his tent by his standard. Each of the twelve tribes of Israel had its own emblem: Judah, a lion; Reuben, a man; Dan, an eagle; Ephraim, an ox; etc.

The Chaldeans used for an emblem a dove standing on a naked sword. Xenophon says that the Persians of his time (400 B. C.) bore an eagle, with wings displayed, on the end of a long lance. The disk of the sun was an ancient Persian emblem also. When the rays of the morning sun struck the brazen standard in front of the general's tent it was the signal to march. The emblems of modern Persia are the lion and the sun. The Parthians employed the figure of a dragon as an emblem. The serpent was a common emblem among heathen tribes.

FIG. 15.—An eagle displayed. Single-headed eagles are found in the arms of the ancient Roman Empire, France, Prussia, etc.; double-headed eagles in the arms of Russia and Austria. (See Plates VI and VII.)

In the early days of the Roman republic

the troops went into battle bearing a wisp of hay bound to a pole. The standards of the different divisions of the army were various until after the time of Marius (died B. C. 86) when the legions received their eagles. The cohorts and centuries of troops had flags with the general's name embroidered upon them, and these flags were given to the bravest and to the oldest soldiers to carry, and they were sacredly guarded. Whoever lost his flag in battle was put to death.

The flag was the symbol of the majesty of Rome and of the valor and loyalty of all the troops. The Roman soldiers swore their oaths of allegiance on the flags. The reverence and devotion with which the modern soldier regards his flag is a direct consequence of the feeling of the Roman legionary for his standard.

FIG. 16.—Eagle of the Roman Legions. S. P. Q. R. stands for Senatus Populusque Quirites Romanus — i. e., the senate and the people of Rome, and the Quirites, who were those Sabines that became Roman citizens.

The idea of the Roman soldier has descended to us and become our inheritance, just as the ideas of duty and of law of the Roman citizen have been transmitted through centuries and adopted in our private and public conduct.

You can read in your Cæsar's Commentaries (Book IV, chapter xxix), how one morn-

Fig. 17.—Eagle of the Roman Legions.

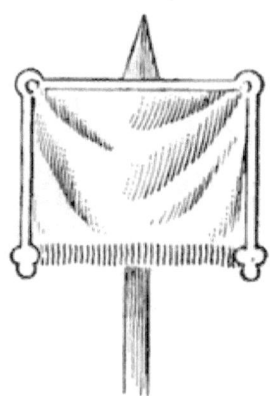

Fig. 18.—A Roman banner or standard.

ing, early, Cæsar found himself under the cliffs of Albion. The Britons of Kent were gathered on the beach to oppose his landing by force. Two hours after noon the preparations of the Romans were all made and the landing was attempted. The ships were so large that they could not come close to the shore, and the heavily armed legionaries had to leap into the sea and there to fight the waves and the enemy.

"Our men," says Cæsar, "with all these things against them were not so alert at fighting as was usual with them on dry ground." Then the eagle bearer of the tenth legion—Cæsar's favorite legion — jumped into the sea, proclaiming that he, at least, would do his duty. Unless they wished to see their eagle fall into the hands of the enemy they must follow him.

"Jump down," he said, "my fellow soldiers, unless you wish to betray your eagle to the enemy. I, at any rate, will do my duty to the republic and to our general." When he had said this with a loud voice, he threw himself out of the ship and advanced the eagle against the enemy. Seeing and hearing this, the men leaped forth from that ship and from

FIG. 19.—The standard of the Gauls or of the Goths, who were legionaries of Rome —the cock was their emblem, and was used by France in modern times (1830).

others. There was some sharp fighting, but at length the Britons fled.

In the first centuries of the Christian era the standard of the emperors of Rome was a purple banner hanging from a beam slung crosswise from a long lance. The banner of the early emperors bore the eagle. A color-guard of fifty men carried it before the Cæsar when he took command of his army. It was his personal standard, and represented his imperial power (see Fig. 18).

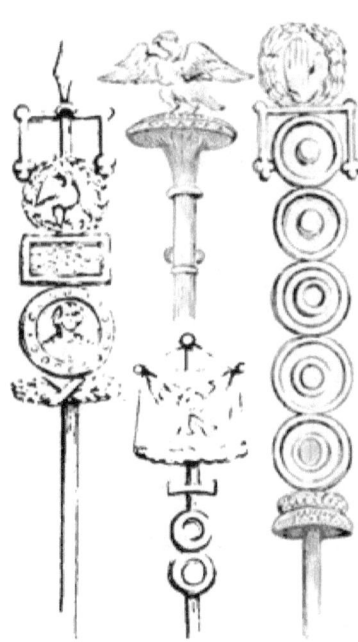

Fig. 20.—Standards of the Roman Legions. The lowest picture shows the monogram, XP, of Christ.

Constantine the Great, before his conversion to Christianity in A. D. 312, bore a banner (called a *lab'arum*) with his likeness and those of his children emblazoned upon it. It was reported that on his conversion he received a new *labarum* as a miraculous gift from Heaven. The point of the lance was replaced by the mono-

gram of Christ XP (Ch, r) in Greek letters*
(see the picture of the *labarum* of Constantine in Fig. 34) and after a time the cross replaced the portrait of the Emperor, and the symbol of Christianity glittered on the helmets of his soldiers and was engraved on their shields.

This was the first Christian banner in Europe. It represented a new idea. The temporal and earthly power of the Emperor was then openly acknowledged to be derived from the spiritual power of Christ. In all Catholic countries to this day the flags of an army are blessed by the priests, and flags captured from the enemy are usually hung in cathedrals.

Fig. 21.—Assyrian standards.

Religious banners came into general use in the early centuries: the blue hood of St. Martin, in the first part of the fifth century, and the *oriflamme* of St. Denis (A. D.

---

* The first two letters of ΧΡΙΣΤΟΣ (Christos).

630), in France; the three banners of St. Peter, St. John of Beverley, St. Wilfred of Ripon, in England (A. D. 1264), and so forth.

We shall hear more about these religious banners when we read the history of the flags of France and England. They came to have places of honor because the spiritual power of the Church was more and more felt to be behind the earthly power of the king. Christ's name on the *labarum* of the Roman Emperor Constantine was the earliest symbol that expressed this belief.

Fig. 22.—Egyptian standard.

The Greeks in the most ancient times carried a piece of armor at the point of a spear before their armies; in later times they displayed standards and banners charged with the emblems of their cities. The emblem of Athens was the owl or the olive. The Lacædemonians used the Greek letters *alpha* (A) or *lambda* (Λ) on their banner. The Thebans adopted the sphinx as an emblem, in memory of Œdipus.*

---

* Œdipus was the King of Thebes who slew the sphinx, according to the legend.

The Corinthians employed the winged horse—Pegasus. Carthage bore a horse's head.

Fig. 23.—Two Mexican standards (ancient).

Such emblems as these have been used by nations and tribes from the most ancient times down to the present day. Trajan's column in Rome was erected in the early years of the second century A. D. The shields of the Dacian warriors that are sculptured upon it bear their personal emblems—the sun, the moon, and so forth.

Our own Red Indian tribes have a *totem*—an emblem—for each clan, and each warrior has his own badge, like a coat of arms. From the very earliest times the white horse was the emblem of the Saxons. It was used by King Alfred the Great (A. D. 900), and is

THE FLAGS OF FOREIGN NATIONS.

Fig. 24.—A dragon *passant*.

Fig. 25.—A wivern.

still the cognizance* of the royal house of Hanover. The kingdom of Wessex bore a golden dragon. The wivern was the emblem of the Vandals; the raven, that of the Danes (see Figs. 24 and 25). The oak is a symbol of strength, the trident of Neptune, and so forth.

Fig. 26.—The "mound." A symbol of imperial or royal power, and of the supreme power of the cross over the world.

In the year 1013 the pope presented to the Emperor Henry II a globe surmounted by a cross to symbolize the power of Christianity and of the cross over the world. The globe without the cross had been em-

---

* The cognizance = the emblem = the heraldic mark by which a family or a person is known.

ployed as a symbol by the Emperor Augustus a thousand years earlier.

There is no emblem more familiar and more sacred than the emblem of the cross. It is far older than Christianity, as we may see (see Fig. 27); but after it was once adopted by the Church as a symbol, it stood for Christianity as the crescent stood for the power of the Saracens.

The Crusades were wars of the cross against the crescent, just as the wars in England (A. D. 1455–'71) between the houses of York (whose emblem was a white rose) and of Lancaster (whose emblem was a red rose) were the Wars of the Roses. Since the world began emblems and symbols like these have represented causes, hopes, aspirations; and men have died under such ban-

FIG. 27.—A Grecian banner. From a mural painting, 500 B. C. Notice that the banner bears the symbol of the cross.

ners for the ideas shadowed forth in the symbols.

Flags that represent national and social ideals are emblems almost as significant as the symbols of religion—the deepest feeling of men's hearts.

It is well worth while to try to understand exactly how a symbol comes to represent—to stand for—an idea. How, for example, the cross really represents Christianity to our thoughts, not merely to our eyes; or how a flag, which is nothing more than a bit of colored cloth to our touch and to our sight, really comes to stand for the idea of our whole country.

Suppose that you try to think of our country, what sort of an idea do you have? You can think of its vast expanse between the two oceans, between the Gulf and the Great Lakes; of the various States and cities, one by one; of the millions of people that inhabit it; of the desires, the hopes, the aspirations of each one out of all these millions; or you can even have an idea of the desires and hopes and aspirations that each person of all the millions has in common with every other one of his fellow countrymen.

It is possible to think each one of these thoughts separately, or even to think them together in a way. These ideas and a hundred more are all included in the notion of "our country."

For instance, when we say "our country," we know, at the very instant, that it is a country devoted to freedom, obedient to law; that it has a character of its own just as a person has a character. We think of its freedom, or of its obedience to law, as part of our country's *character*, just as we feel that one of our friends is kind, and truthful, and courageous, and trustworthy.

All such separate facts go to make up the character of our friend; and the idea of our country contains a thousand separate facts of the same sort. Our country is like a person. And just as we feel that one of our friends has a certain character and would act in a certain way if he were tried in certain circumstances, so we feel that our country has a character; that it is more than a vast expanse of land, more than millions of separate people; that it has desires, and virtues, and faults, and hopes, and aspirations of its very own that make it what it really is.

When we look at a photograph of our friend, or when we speak his name, we are vividly reminded of his character. And when we speak the name of our country— America—or when we see its flag waving in the breeze, we seem to know the country as a whole. The word America and the flag, are symbols that imply its *whole* character. Back of the word that can be heard, or of the flag that can be touched, there is an idea which either of these symbols serves to call up in our minds.

Whenever we see the flag it stands for the whole country and for the whole of the country, just as the name America stands for every part of our national character—for its bravery, its honor, its kindness, its energy, its devotion to law, its obedience to order.

The flag is a symbol of the whole country and represents its character. When we see this symbol we know our country just as we know our friend when we hear his name spoken. As years go on we know our friend better and better. We become more and more acquainted with his virtues, and we find new excellences in him. He still has the same name; but this name comes to mean more and more to us as we understand him better. The form of the symbol (his name) remains the same, but it stands for more and for different things. It is the same with the name of a country, or with its flag.

As we learn to understand better and better what the character of a country really is, the symbols that represent it take on new meanings. The symbols themselves usually remain unchanged in form; but they stand for new things. Some symbols have a long history. The cross now stands for Christianity and represents the whole Christian history. But the symbol is far older than the Christian era. It has come to represent a new thing. It is very instructive to trace the history of any symbol of the sort. It helps us to understand the impulses that move the minds of men. Let us take a few examples of symbols with long histories.

Learned men have proved, by ways that are too complicated to be written out in this little book, that the two symbols in Figs. 28 and 29 mean much the same thing, and have much the same history.

If we should stop to write out the proofs that the learned men used, this chapter would be very long and rather uninteresting. But if you will take their proofs for granted and only pay attention to the things that they have found out, you will not think what they say uninteresting at all. On the contrary, you will begin to see what wonderful things symbols are, and how they have a kind of life of their own. These two symbols have lived for at least thirty centuries, and they are young still, and will live much longer yet.

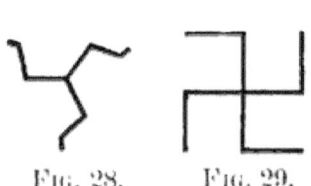

Fig. 28.   Fig. 29.

The symbol of a kind of cross with three points was used centuries ago to represent the motions of the sun in the heavens in its daily course from rising to setting. People looked on the sun as the source of all the life of plants and beasts and of men, as indeed it is in a way. They did not look farther than the sun for a God who created it; they thought of the Sun himself as a god, and they represented his course in the heavens by this three-legged cross.

One of the arms of the cross represented

the morning sun, one the sun at noon, and the other the sun in the afternoon. The three arms together pointed out the whole journey of the Sun in the heavens: the daily miracle of his rising, his culmination, his setting.

This symbol was known in Eastern countries for a very long time before the Christian era begins. The first time that it appeared in the West was on the coins of Lycia,* about four hundred and eighty years before Christ. All the nations and cities about the Mediterranean Sea were trading with each other, and the symbols of one country or tribe were known to other tribes or countries in the neighborhood. Coins, especially, would pass from hand to hand. Now, Sicily was a fertile country engaged in trade. Ceres, the patron goddess of agriculture, was born in Sicily, and the ancient name of Sicily was the land of the three capes (*Trinakria*).

Some Sicilian sailor, or merchant, or lawgiver, saw one of these coins of Lycia, and it seemed to him that this curious device of a three-armed cross was precisely the symbol

---

* Lycia was a province of Asia Minor bordering on the Mediterranean Sea.

for his own country of three capes; there was an arm for each cape. So, as early as B. C. 317, the coins of Sicily bear the three-armed cross as a symbol. It was a symbol of the three capes, and no longer a reminder of the course of the Sun-God in the heavens.

The Crusades brought many English and Scottish knights to Oriental countries and to Sicily, between the date of the first Crusade (A. D. 1095) and of the last (1270). It was just at the time of the Crusades that warriors began to assume coats of arms as marks of knightly bravery and distinction, and it is about this time that the three-armed cross first appears in the coats of arms of English families. The Crusaders totally lost sight of the real meaning of the symbol, and took the three arms of the cross to be three human legs, as in the picture. They were the three legs of a man; and in the year 1266 this symbol was introduced into the Isle of Man, near England, and to this day forms a part of the coat of arms of that province.

Fig. 30.—The three-armed cross of the arms of the Isle of Man.

Here is a symbol that has preserved its

form for centuries, though its early meanings were soon lost. It was never a sacred symbol to the Crusaders or even to the Sicilians; but its shape has been preserved, like that of a fly in amber, for centuries. So long as coats of arms continue to be used, it will remain an English heraldic device.*

The three-armed cross is only a special form of the four-armed cross shown in the last picture. This was likewise a symbol of the sun in very early times, though it has now quite lost this meaning. The learned men tell us that this symbol was found in the Troad—on the plain of Troy—at least thirteen centuries before Christ — that is, thirty-two hundred years ago.

It was known in Greece twelve centuries before Christ; in India and in Sicily, three centuries before Christ; in Britain, about the beginning of the Christian era; in China, Persia, North Africa, Europe, about the same time; in Tibet, a few hundred years later; and it had penetrated to remote Iceland by the ninth century.

It stood for a symbol of the sun in the

---

* See the paragraph Korea in Chapter V for another example of a very ancient symbol still in use.

beginning; for a symbol of the religion of Buddha, in India and Japan; and for a symbol of Christianity in European countries. Its form remained unchanged, but its meaning varied. Men used it to symbolize their beliefs, as these slowly changed through many centuries, from heathenism to Christianity. Whatever the belief of any century may have been, there was a symbol ready at hand to stand for it.

To the heathen it was a symbol of the sun; to the Oriental, a symbol of Buddha; to the European, a symbol of Christ, who died on the cross. In every land it was reverenced. The Japanese Buddhist to-day sees in it a reminder of the founder of his religion, just as the Christian sees in it a reminder of Christ's sufferings. It is a sacred symbol to both; it represents a world of ideas; it embodies a belief.

The flag of a country is a symbol of the same sort. A flag stands for the personality of a country, for its character, its virtues, its hopes, its aspirations. Men die for a flag to uphold the ideals that are embodied in their country, just as thousands of martyrs have died for the cross.

The picture that follows gives a few of the many forms of the cross since it became a Christian symbol. In the very first centuries after Christ the favorite symbol of the Christians was a *fish*, not the cross. The Greek name for a fish is IΧΘΥΣ, and the let-

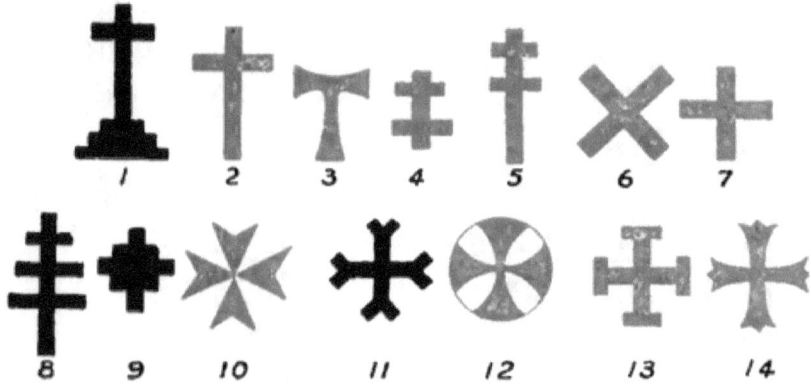

Fig. 31.—Some of the many forms of crosses: 1, Cross of Calvary; 2, Latin cross; 3, Tau-cross (like the Greek letter *tau*); 4, Lorraine cross; 5, Patriarchal cross; 6, St. Andrew's cross (the Scottish cross); 7, St. George's cross (the English cross)—it is also called the Greek cross; 8, Papal cross (its three arms symbolize the ecclesiastical, the civil, and the judicial jurisdictions of the pope); 9, cross nowy-quadrant; 10, the cross of Malta; 11, cross fourché (that is, forked); 12, cross formé or cross patté; 13, cross potent (the cross in the ancient arms of Jerusalem); 14, cross flory.

ters of this word make the initials of the Greek phrase "Jesus Christ, the Son of God, the Saviour." The fish was the favorite Christian symbol until the tenth century.

The cross was always one of the symbols of Christianity, but after that time it became the chief among all. After the sixth century the cross began to be drawn in the very shape of the cross of the crucifixion (Fig. 1 of the picture), and it thus became an *image*, something different from a symbol.

A victorious nation often adopts, with a changed meaning, the symbols of the conquered. Symbols travel from land to land, and they are fossil history. The Franks—the French—took the eagle of the Romans. The Romans took the dragon from the barbarians, and in later times the Normans took the dragon symbol from the Romans themselves. The last chapters of this book give brief histories of the flags of the sovereign states of the world—that is, of the symbols which nations have chosen to represent their nationality. The history of the flags of Denmark, England, France, Japan, Würtemberg, among others, will serve to illustrate by historical examples what has just been said about symbols.

Every knight of the times of chivalry bore a flag of some sort. Those of the lower ranks carried a *pennon* (see *B* of Fig. 34) on the end of a lance. A knight banneret was of higher rank and carried a square *banner* (see *C* of Fig. 34) which was sometimes hung from a lance, but often was attached to a trumpet. As Shakespeare says:

"*I will a banner from a trumpet take
And use it for my haste.*"

Standards were much larger flags and were only borne by kings, princes, commanders in chief, or by the higher nobles. They were huge flags several yards long (see *D* of Fig. 34). The *bandrol* was a small banner, and the *penoncel* or *pensil*, a small narrow pennon. In Sir Walter Scott's poem of Marmion he describes (in canto iv) the camp of Scotland before the battle of Flodden, with its wilderness of tents, each marked by the banner of some knight—

"*A thousand streamers flaunted fair:
Various in shape, device and hue—
Green, sanguine,* purple, red and blue,
Broad, narrow, swallow-tailed and square,
Scroll, pennon, pensil, bandrol,† there
O'er the pavilions ‡ flew.*"

---

* The color of blood.
† Ancient forms of flags.
‡ Pavilions = large tents.

> Highest and midmost was descried
> The royal banner, floating wide;
> The staff, a pine tree strong and straight,
> Pitched deeply in a massive stone,
> Which still in memory is shown.*
> Yet beneath the standard's weight,
> Whene'er the western wind unrolled,
> With toil, the huge and cumbrous fold,
> And gave to view the dazzling field,
> Where, in proud Scotland's royal shield,
> The ruddy lion ramped in gold." †

The flag, the ensign, was in Shakespeare's time called "the ancient," and the same term designated the officer, the ensign, who bore the banner.

> "——more ragged than an old-faced ancient (ensign)."
> —*First part of King Henry IV, iv, 2.*

Speaking of Iago, it is said:

> "This is Othello's ancient (ensign) as I take it."
> —*Othello, c, 1.*

Our knowledge of the forms of antique flags and banners is derived chiefly from old paintings and illuminated manuscripts, and

---

* Which is still to this day shown as a memorial.

† A red lion, rampant, on a gold field is the arms of Scotland (see the upper right-hand colored flag in Plate III).

from a very remarkable piece of needlework, "the Bayeux tapestry," that has been preserved to this day. It is said to have been worked by Matilda, Queen of William the Conqueror, and by the ladies of her court.

FIG. 32.—Two figures from the Bayeux tapestry. Notice the form of the flag and the symbol that it bears.

However this may be, it is certain that the tapestry is very old, and that it represents the history of England from the time of King Harold's visit to the Norman court till his death at the battle of Hastings in 1066. The tapestry is nineteen inches wide and more than two hundred feet long, and contains something over ten thousand separate figures of ships, castles, warriors, flags, horses, dogs, etc. The flags are mostly of the pennon form, and they usually have three points to the tail. They are covered with the emblems of the warriors, and it is from just such emblems that the heraldry of the Crusades took its symbols. The war ships of the Middle Ages bore emblems on their sails as in the accompanying illustration.

Fig. 33.—Ancient war ships with banners on their sails.

CHAPTER IV.

THE FLAGS OF FOREIGN NATIONS—ENGLAND—SIGNALING BY FLAGS—SALUTES—FRANCE.

The history of the flags of England and of France will be given with some fullness. England has an historic relation with America, and her story is in some sense our own. The variations that have occurred in the banners of France during the past fourteen hundred years illustrate in the most complete way the manner in which the symbols of a nation may alter as their national ideals and institutions change. Even for these two ensigns only an outline history can be given; there is no room for more.

Other national flags are referred to in Chapter V in short paragraphs that give the most interesting facts regarding them. The colored plates throughout the book illustrate what is said in the text, and they should be constantly consulted.

The reader must not forget that each and every one of these flags has a long and eventful history. A flag is, and always has been, a symbol of beliefs and aspirations. As these have changed the symbols have usually changed with them. Sometimes a changed belief is fitted to an ancient symbol, as we saw in Chapter III. If we have leisure to study any set of symbols whatever, we shall always find warm human life back of them. The history of any man or of any nation, with its beliefs, its actions, its passions, its joys, its sorrows, its successes and misfortunes, is always full of interest. The symbols of such a history are only uninteresting when we are ignorant of their meaning.

Nothing can be less interesting than the flag of Bulgaria, for instance, to one who is ignorant of her long history. But if you know the relations of the Bulgarian nation to the Roman Empire, the wars of the kingdom of Bulgaria with the Empire of the East, the conversion of the Bulgarians to Greek Christianity, their centuries of suffering under Turkish rule, their release from that rule by Russian intervention, and their recent struggles to form an independent state, you will see an historic continuity in it all, and the new flag of Bulgaria will come to have a deep meaning. (See Plate VIII and Chapter V.)

THE FLAGS OF ENGLAND.

William the Conqueror, Duke of Normandy, invaded England in the year 1066, and defeated the Saxons at the battle of Hastings. The standard of the Saxons at that memorable battle was a dragon standard. It was not a painted banner, nor a sculptured image, but a floating figure in the shape of a dragon made of cloth. The wind filled the double walls of the figure, which was made like a bag, and the standard appeared solid and lifelike. Such dragon standards had been used on the Continent of Europe long before this time, and they are employed in China and other eastern countries to this day.

The banner of William the Conqueror was sent to him by the pope. It was a white banner bordered with blue, and it bore a golden cross. It is figured on the Bayeux tapestry (see Fig. 32).

Richard the Lion-hearted, King of England, displayed a dragon standard in 1191, and it was in use in England as late as 1264, and by English armies on the Continent during the fourteenth century. King Henry III, in 1244, gave an order for the making of a standard. It was to portray "a dragon, of red silk sparkling all over with fine gold, the tongue to resemble burning fire, and the eyes to be of sapphires."

The standards of early times were huge affairs, and they were often set up in the midst of a chariot drawn by oxen or horses. The Italians of Milan, in 1035 A. D., carried the banner of their city in this fashion on a red car supporting a red mast with a gilded ball at the top. The banner floated from a pole hung crosswise from the mast. In 1138 King Stephen of England had such a chariot. It supported a mast carrying a silver pyx,* and the pyx contained a consecrated wafer of the Blessed Sacrament. In 1264 a chariot of the sort displayed from its mast the three sacred banners of St. Peter, St. John of Beverley, St. Wilfred of Ripon—three patron saints of England.

---

* The pyx is the box or vase used to contain the consecrated wafer of the Holy Sacrament.

The banners and standards of the Western world were profoundly changed by the wars of the Crusades. Heraldry—the set of rules governing the use of emblems, badges, coats of arms, flags, and all honorary distinctions—grew into form during the Crusades. It was found to be a useful and even a necessary thing to have a kind of a science or doctrine of the sort in the huge crusading armies where men of many nations were gathered together.

Emblems of one sort or another had been used from the earliest times, as we have said. A badge was employed to distinguish the little band of soldiers who obeyed a single chief. The chief himself had his own personal banner or flag. The Crusaders of different nations were distinguished by crosses of different colors sewed on the surcoats that covered their armor. The English bore a white cross, and the French a red cross, for instance.

The white cross continued to be the cross of Englishmen during the Crusades, but it was changed soon afterward. During all their wars in France under the Black Prince, and during the fifteenth century, the English cross was red and the French cross white. In a miniature showing King John of France as a prisoner of King Edward III of England (about 1350), the French king holds in his hand a little red flag with a white cross, and the King of England holds a white flag with a red cross—the cross of St. George.

During the third Crusade (1189) coats of arms were usually borne by all the great nobles. They had proved to be useful in time of battle. The knight could be distinguished in the press of men by the high crest on his helmet, by the coat of arms emblazoned on his shield or on the trappings of his war horse. His followers and retainers wore his badge or emblem. His banner was embroidered or painted with his armorial bearings.

When King Richard, the Lion-hearted, returned from Palestine (1194), the three lions (often called leopards) of his coat of arms became the royal arms of England. They are shown on the first and third quarters of the royal banner of Great Britain in Plate III.

The royal arms of Great Britain and Ireland fill the four quarters of that banner. The arms of the separate countries are shown on the royal standard thus:

      I. England.   II. Scotland.
      III. Ireland.   IV. England.

Wales was joined to England in 1283, and does not appear in the arms. Scotland's arms entered in 1603, at the time of the union, and Ireland's entered at the same time, though the act of union for Ireland was not passed by the Parliament until 1801.

The royal banner of Scotland, a red lion rampant on a golden field, within a double tressure flory-counter-flory, is separately shown in Plate III. The royal arms of Scotland are very ancient. The lion is borne within a double tressure ornamented with fleurs-de-lis. It is said that these were added to record the alliances between the French and Scottish kings. The cognizance of Ireland is comparatively modern. It is a golden harp with silver strings on an azure field (see Plate III). Its flag has a green field.

King Edward III of England claimed the kingship of France. By virtue of his descent from his mother, a French princess, and added fleurs-de-lis to the royal arms to mark his claim. The fleurs-de-lis were the royal arms of France. They were borne by all English kings from 1340 until 1801, although the English lost all their French possessions (except the town of Calais) as early as 1431.

The royal banner of England is a personal standard, not the flag of the country. The flag of Englishmen is the banner of St. George, a red cross on a white field (Fig. 3 and Fig. 35). There are legends relating how this saint rendered great aid and service to King Richard, the Lion-hearted, who placed himself and the English army under the saint's protection; and during the twelfth century St. George became the patron saint of England. From the year 1222 onward, his feast day was regularly kept as a holiday. The dragon of St. George is a pagan myth, adopted and made over anew.

St. George of England has a church dedicated to him in Rome (San Georgio de Velabro), and his banner of red silk is still displayed there once in every year. St. George is also the patron saint of Russia, and his symbol (the saint overcoming a dragon) is borne on the royal coat of arms. Plate VII

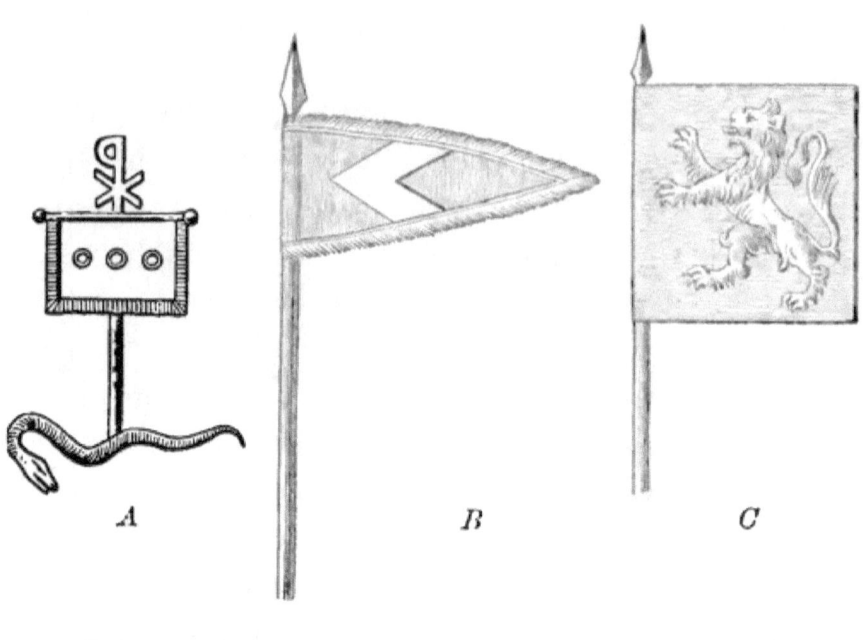
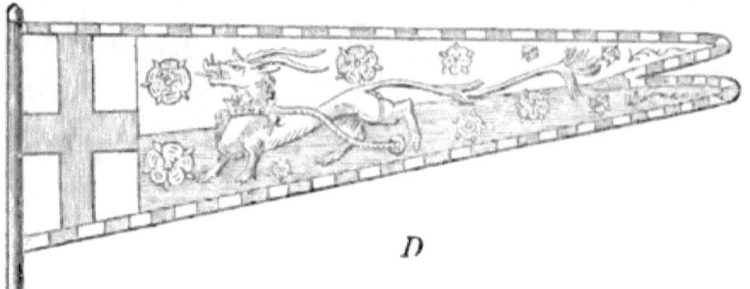

Fig. 34.—Various forms of early standards and banners. *A* = the *labarum* of the Emperor Constantine (A. D. 312). The monogram of Christ is at the head of the staff, above the banner, and below it is a serpent. *B* = the pennon of a knight of the Middle Ages; it is a blue pennon with a silver chevron. *C* = a banner of the Middle Ages—a lion rampant on a blue field. *D* = the royal standard of King Henry V of England, who reigned from 1413 to 1422. The standard was eleven yards long; the cross of St. George is displayed for England, and the ancient dragon also; the roses are emblems of the House of Lancaster; the upper half of the standard is white, the lower blue, and the border is white and blue.

shows the effigy of St. George and the dragon on the red shield in the center of the Russian imperial standard.

The legend of St. Andrew's cross declares that a white cross appeared on the blue sky during a famous battle of the year 940, when the Scots and Picts defeated the English and left their King Athelstane dead on the field. A better opinion is that it was adopted as the Scottish symbol in the time of the early Crusades (thirteenth century). It is exceedingly doubtful whether St. Andrew was crucified on a cross of this shape, as the legends declare; and St. Patrick was not crucified at all, though a saltire has been attributed as his symbol also.

Ireland was united with Great Britain (that is, with England, Wales, and Scotland) in 1801, and the cross of St. Patrick was added to the old Union Jack to form the present one. The Union Jack is composed of the symbols of three saints; and it is to this day the royal colors. It is displayed on all ships of war, by every regiment, and at every fortress. The main changes in English flags are shown in the pictures that have been given. There have been other changes from time to time that are of interest to Englishmen, but not to Americans.

The royal standard since the time of King Richard I (1194) has always borne the coat of arms of the reigning monarch. This coat has changed from time to time as kings of different houses have sat upon the throne (the Plantagenets, 1154 to 1399; the house of Lancaster, 1399 to 1461; the house of York, 1461 to 1485; the house of Tudor, 1485 to 1603; the house of Stuart, 1603 to 1649, and from 1660 to 1714; the Commonwealth, from 1649 to 1660; the house of Hanover, from 1714 to the present day).

The Union Jack was declared to be the king's colors in 1606. On British men-of-war it is displayed from a jack staff in the bow of the ship, and American war vessels have adopted the same custom and fly their jack (Plate II) in the same way.

It is believed that the term "Jack" is derived from the abbreviated name of the reigning sovereign, King James I, under whose direction the first Union Flag was constructed, and who signed his name "Jacques."

The white ensign with St. George's cross

has been the real flag of the English people since the end of the twelfth century. It was a part of the royal standard in early times, as, for example, in the drawing, Fig. 34, of the standard of Henry V (1413–'22), and it is now the distinctive flag of Her Majesty's ships of war, etc.

For a time the war ships flew three different ensigns—namely, the white ensign (the cross of St. George); the red ensign (a red flag with the Union Jack on a canton); and the blue ensign (a blue flag with the Union Jack on a canton) (see Plate III for the present form of these flags). Nelson's fleet was divided into "red," "white," and "blue" squadrons; and in histories of that time one reads of "Admirals of the Blue," etc.—that is, admirals commanding the division with the blue flag, etc.

All British ships of war now fly the white ensign. The blue ensign is displayed by all vessels of the naval reserve—that is, by all merchant vessels that are liable to be called into service as auxiliary cruisers, scouts, or troop ships in time of war. The Cunard steamers, for example, fly this flag. They are merchant vessels in time of peace, and

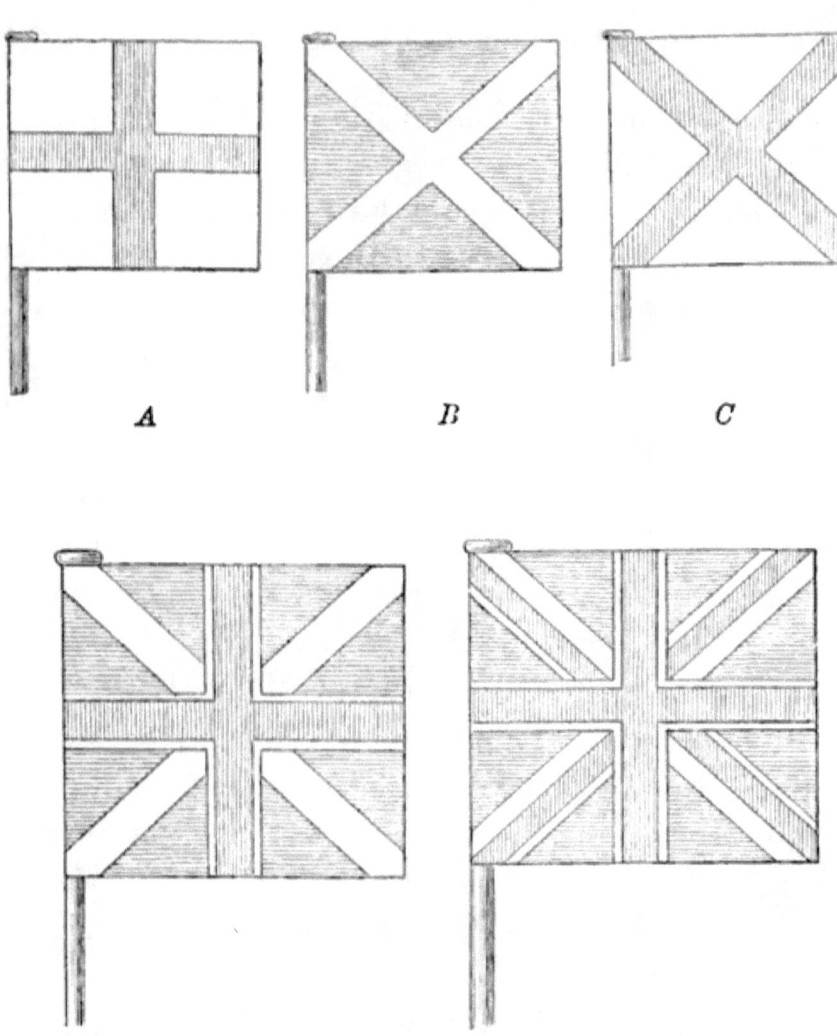

Fig. 35.—Flags of Great Britain. $A =$ the cross of St. George for England (a red cross on a white field); $B =$ the cross of St. Andrew for Scotland (a white saltire on a blue field); $C =$ the cross of St. Patrick for Ireland (a red saltire on a white field); $D =$ the Union Jack in 1606; $E =$ the Union Jack at the present time (see Figs. 3, 4, and 5).

can be called into the service of the navy in time of war. British yachts fly the blue ensign. The red ensign ("the meteor flag of England") is now distinctively the flag of their merchant service. It may be seen in every port in the world.

The emblems of England, Scotland, and Ireland are respectively the rose, the thistle, and the shamrock (a trefoil, a clover leaf). The rose was assumed as a personal emblem by Edward I (reigned 901–925). The red rose of the house of Lancaster and the white of the house of York were the symbols of the two parties in the famous Wars of the Roses (1455–'71).

The thistle of Scotland is said to have been adopted as a symbol because a party of invading Danes, in the early part of the eleventh century, cried out as they stepped on a bed of thistles, and were thus discovered and defeated. The shamrock was used, it is said, by St. Patrick, in the fifth century, to illustrate the mystery of the Trinity to his Irish converts to Christianity. He showed them its three leaves united on one stem to explain the mystery of three Persons and one God.

SIGNALING BY FLAGS.

Merchant vessels always carry a set of signal flags (see Plate IV). There are about twenty flags in a set. Each ship has a code book or dictionary of signals also. This is a book with the pages arranged in two columns, one of words and another of numbers corresponding to the words. The specimen that follows is not a part of the code in actual use, but is intended to explain in a simple way how such a book is arranged.

Words.	Numbers.	Words.	Numbers.
Any	0172	Longitude	3300
Are	0217	My	3318
Boston	0324	Of	3625
Bound	0410	On	3697
Fire	1873	Provisions	4114
For	1927	Ship	4308
Have	2722	Short	4413
Is	2984	We	4811
Latitude	3000	Where	4916
Letters	3267	You	5004

Ten of the signal flags stand for the ten digits, 0, 1, 2, 3, 4, 5, 6, 7, 8, 9; and flags also stand for single letters of the alphabet (see Plate IV) so that words can be spelled out, letter by letter.

When two ships meet they first show the

ensigns of their countries, the American and British flags, for instance. Then the American ship hoists a set of flags that make a number, like 1720. In a printed list of American merchant vessels opposite the number 1720, the British captain finds the *name* of the American ship—as, 1720 = the ship Confidence, of Boston. The British ship hoists her number also, and the American captain finds in a list of British vessels the name of the British ship—as, 7840 = the bark Alliance, of Liverpool.

Messages can now be exchanged by using the code book. For instance, the American can ask the British ship, "Have you any letters for Boston?" by hoisting the signal flags that give the numbers standing opposite to these words in the code book; thus, 2722—5004—0172—3267—1927—0324. "We are short of provisions," could be sent by displaying the numbers 4811—0217—4413—3625—4114; "My ship is on fire," by 3318—4308—2984—3697—1873; "What is your longitude and latitude?" etc. Any desired message can be sent in this way.

In the code in actual use the flags PH mean "We are starving"; NM means "The ship is on fire"; BRS stands for "Will you take a letter for me?" DWHB means "Surrender your ship at once"; and so forth. There are several thousand such phrases in the book, and they cover nearly all the questions and answers in common use.

If you will look in the shipping news of a daily newspaper you will see such entries as this, "Spoken by the British ship Alliance, of Liverpool, on June 17th, in longitude 30° W., latitude, 50° N., the American ship Confidence, of Boston, bound for Barbadoes. All well." Every ship reports the vessels she has "spoken" during her voyage the moment she arrives at a port, and in this way the movements of merchant vessels are known to their owners. Colored lights ready prepared to show the colors of the different flags are used at night. A blue and red flag is represented by a blue and red light, etc.

The account that has just been given is intended to explain the principle on which marine signaling is conducted, rather than to give the details of how the signals are sent in actual practice. In practice, a message is announced by hoisting the code pennant (the last pennant of Plate IV) below the national ensign. The vessel that is to receive the message hoists the same pennant as an answering pennant, to show that she understands. The message is then sent by numbers or by letters according to the special code in use. There are no vowels in the flag alphabet except *a*, which is denoted by the code pennant. The flag signals alone are difficult to read at sea, and a better system is to use black balls with a few very simple and plain flags. All of these matters are treated of in special books on signals.

The war ships of each nation have a secret code of their own, and every such ship has a signal officer. The signal book itself has lead all around its covers, so that if it is thrown into the sea it will sink and its secrets will still be preserved. A war ship surrendering to the enemy would take this way of guarding the code, and it might be necessary in case of wreck or of fire. The signal 250, "The enemy is escaping," was the first one hoisted by the American fleet at Santiago de Cuba on July 3, 1898, when the Spanish fleet was destroyed. Beside the naval code the open international code just described is used by the vessels of every nation—war vessels and merchant ships alike.

It is quite unnecessary to go into details regarding signal codes by flags, but there are a few things every one should know. Flags speak a universal language that any one may read. Suppose you are in the lower bay of New York city watching a great steamer coming in. She is an English ship, because she carries the ensign of England from a staff over her stern.* She is bound for an American port, and the American ensign at her foremast head tells that fact to every one. At her mainmast head she flies the private flag of her owners. It is usually a *burgee*—that is, a triangular pennant with a swallow-tail end. The house flag of the Cunard line is red and bears a gold lion; the American line flies a white flag with a blue eagle displayed, and so on. Each steamship line has its own house flag, of course.

If she wants a tugboat to tow her to her landing place she will fly the national ensign

---

* A Cunard steamer will carry the *blue* ensign because she is in the naval reserve of England—usually the red ensign is flown by merchant vessels.

110   THE FLAGS OF FOREIGN NATIONS.

halfway up her main rigging. Each nation has its own pilot flag. For the United States it is "the jack," for England the union

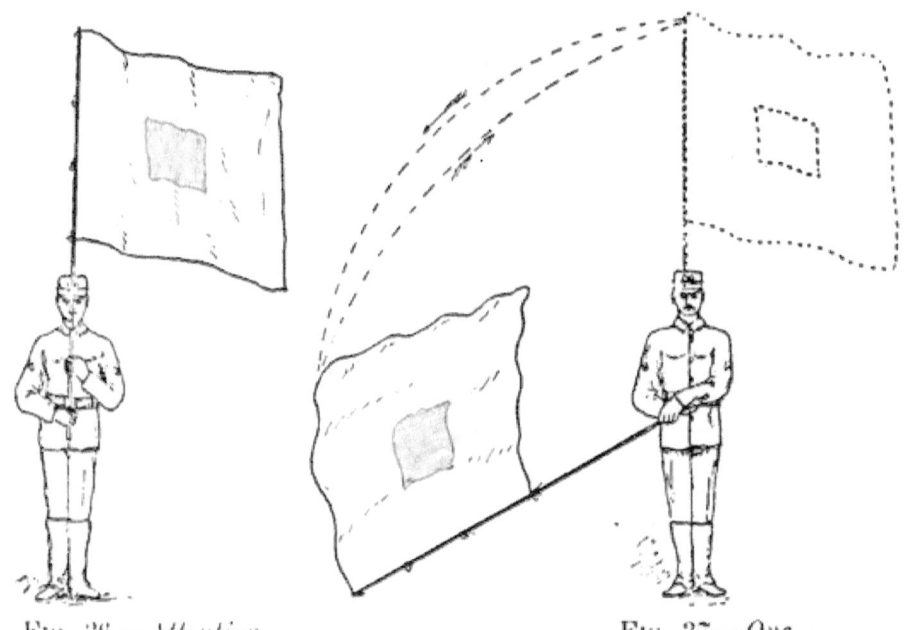

Fig. 36.—*Attention*.   Fig. 37.—*One*.

jack; and when a pilot is needed it is displayed at the foremast head. United States men-of-war fly the jack at a little staff near the bow of the vessel whenever the ship is in order and ready for fighting or inspection.

A ship at anchor in the harbor might be seen to display a yellow flag. This would mean that she had illness among her people, that she was in quarantine.* If her flag is red, she is taking on powder or other danger-

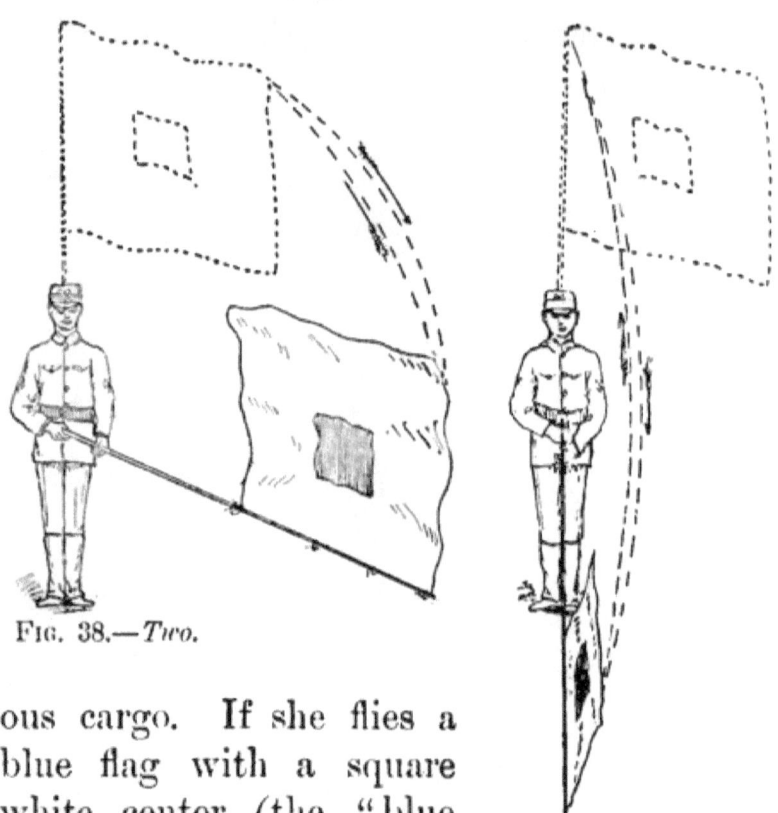

Fig. 38.—*Two.*

Fig. 39.—*Three.*

ous cargo. If she flies a blue flag with a square white center (the "blue Peter" so-called) it means she is about to sail—she will sail that very day—and mails and luggage must be hurried on board.

---

* In old times such ships were detained for forty days. *Quarante* is the French for forty, and quarant-ine the term derived from it.

In the army (and also in the navy) messages can be sent by spelling out words from signals made by waving a flag to the right or left, as follows: A flag some four feet square is fastened to a staff some eight feet long. The flag is held vertically in front of the person sending the signals, except at the moment when the letters are formed (Fig. 36). When the flag is waved once from the vertical position to the *right* and back again, the motion stands for 1 (Fig. 37). When the flag is waved once from the vertical position to the *left* and back again, the motion stands for 2 (Fig. 38). When the flag is waved once from the vertical position to the *front* and back again, the motion stands for 3 (Fig. 39).

An alphabet can now be arranged as follows:

A = 22	J = 1122	S = 212
B = 2112	K = 2121	T = 2
C = 121	L = 221	U = 112
D = 222	M = 1221	V = 1222
E = 12	N = 11	W = 1121
F = 2221	O = 21	X = 2122
G = 2211	P = 1212	Y = 111
H = 122	Q = 1211	Z = 2222
I = 1	R = 211	

end of a word = 3
end of a sentence = 33
end of a message = 333

NUMERALS.

```
1.................................1111
2.................................2222
3.................................1112
4.................................2221
5.................................1122
6.................................2211
7.................................1222
8.................................2111
9.................................1221
0.................................2112
```

A message can be sent by spelling out the words, as follows:

```
The   = 2—122—12—3,
Army  = 22—211—1221—111—3,
Moves = 1221—21—1222—12—212—3,
To    = 2—21—3,
Day   = 222—22—111—333.
```

Signals like these can be read at a considerable distance, especially if field glasses are employed. Messages in the Morse code of telegraphy can be sent by making 1 = a dot, 2 = a dash, 3 = a long dash, etc. Lights are employed at night in place of the flags, using a red light for 1 and a white light for 2. The beams from an electric search light or the sounds of a steam whistle can be used for the same purpose and in much the same way.

The Morse Telegraph Code.

ALPHABET.

A ·—	F ··—·	K —·—	P ·——·	U ··—
B —···	G ——·	L ——	Q ···—·	V ···—
C ··· ·	H ····	M ——	R ·· ·	W ·——
D —··	I ··	N —·	S ···	X ·—··
E ·	J —·—·	O · ·	T —	Y ·· ··
		Z ··· ·	& · ···	

NUMERALS.

1 ·——·	3 ···—·	5 ———	7 ——· ·	9 —···
2 · —··	4 ····—	6 ······	8 —····	0 ——

Any energetic boy can get a great deal of pleasure and advantage out of signaling by flags. All he has to do is to set up a flagpole on the top of his house where it can be seen by other boys of his acquaintance. It is not much trouble to make a few flags and to arrange a code of signals with his friends. A white flag with a blue center might mean "football on next Saturday"; and a blue flag with a white center, "I can not come out to-day," etc. If he will learn the army code of signaling by flags he can send long messages.

The most memorable signal ever displayed was flown from the flagship of Admiral Nelson—the Victory—on October 21, 1805, just before going into action against the combined fleets of France and Spain. Nelson commanded a British fleet of twenty-seven ships. The enemy's force was thirty-three ships. The odds were against the English. Nelson was the bravest and best of commanders, and his men had perfect trust in him. His signal expressed the proud con-

FIG. 40.—Nelson's signal before going into action at the battle of Trafalgar—England expects every man will do his duty.

fidence of the commander in chief and of the country at home in "every man" of the British fleet. *England expects that every man will do his duty.** The trust was justified.

---

* In this message the emphasis is on *every*, and not on *duty*, as it is often incorrectly spoken.

At the end of the battle nineteen of the enemy's ships had been captured or destroyed, and the power of France on the sea annihilated. Nelson's signal is the full expression of the spirit in which great deeds are done.

UNITED STATES WEATHER BUREAU SIGNALS.

In most cities of the United States the local observer of the Weather Service displays signals to indicate the probabilities as to coming weather and winds.

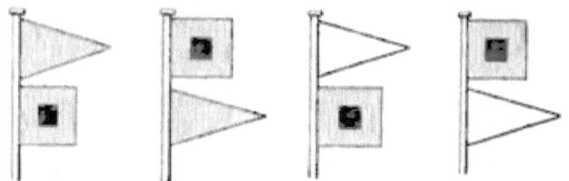

N. E. winds. S. E. winds. N. W. winds. S. W. winds.

FIG. 41.—Storm signals.

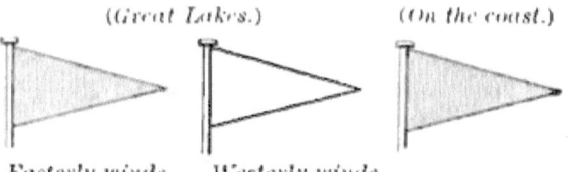

(Great Lakes.)   (On the coast.)

Easterly winds. Westerly winds.

FIG. 42.—Information signals.

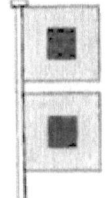

FIG. 43.—Hurricane signal.

Explanation of Storm, Information, and Hurricane Signals.

Storm Signal.—A red flag with a black center indicates that a storm of marked violence is expected.

The pennants displayed with the flags indicate the direction of the wind; red, *easterly* (from northeast to south); white, *westerly* (from southwest to north). The pennant above the flag indicates that the wind is expected to blow from the northerly quadrants; below, from the southerly quadrants.

By night a red light indicates *easterly* winds, and a white light above a red light, *westerly* winds.

Information Signal.—(Red or white pennant displayed alone.)—When displayed at stations on the Great Lakes indicates that winds are expected which may prove dangerous to small vessels, the red pennant indicating *easterly* and the white pennant *westerly* winds.

When the red pennant is displayed at stations on the Atlantic, Pacific, and Gulf coasts it indicates that the local observer has received information from the central office of a storm covering a limited area, dangerous only for vessels about to sail to certain points, and serves as a notification to shipmasters that information will be given them upon application to the local observer. Only the red pennant is displayed on the coasts.

Hurricane Signal.—Two red flags with black centers, displayed one above the other, indicate the expected approach of tropical hurricanes, and also of those extremely severe and dangerous storms which occasionally move across the Lakes and northern Atlantic coast.

No night information or hurricane signals are displayed.

WEATHER SIGNALS.

(See Fig. 44.)

Five flags are employed to indicate coming rain, snow, cold waves, and other changes of temperature, as below:

THE FLAGS OF FOREIGN NATIONS.

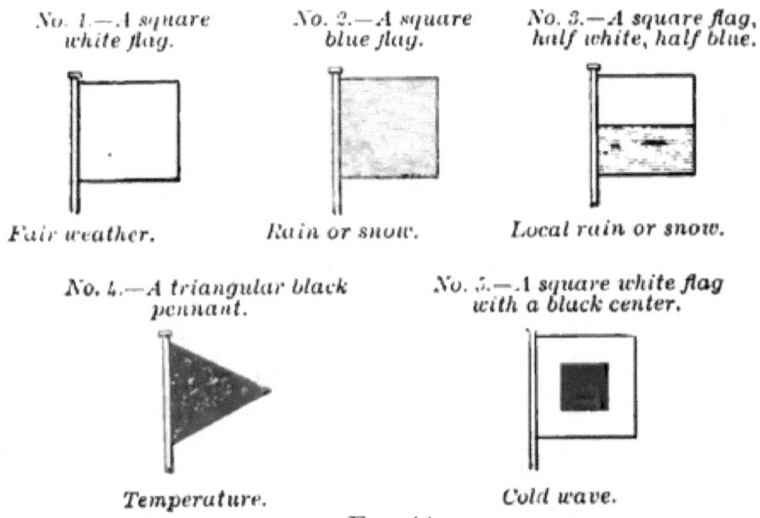

Fig. 44.

INTERPRETATION OF DISPLAYS.

No. 1, alone, indicates fair weather, stationary temperature.

No. 2, alone, indicates rain or snow, stationary temperature.

No. 3, alone, indicates local rain or snow, stationary temperature.

No. 1, with No. 4 above it, indicates fair weather, warmer.

No. 1, with No. 4 below it, indicates fair weather, colder.

No. 2, with No. 4 above it, indicates rain or snow, warmer.

No. 2, with No. 4 below it, indicates rain or snow, colder.

No. 3, with No. 4 above it, indicates local rain or snow, warmer.

No. 3, with No. 4 below it, indicates local rain or snow, colder.

SALUTES.

Salutes are exchanged between vessels at sea or in ports in various ways. In former times the flag was dipped (that is, lowered smoothly to about half mast and quickly hoisted again) and the topsails lowered. Or, the course of the saluting vessel was slightly altered. When the Mayflower was coming to New England in 1620, she met a small French vessel—"when we drew near her, we put forth our ancient,* and she luffed up the wind to us."

England from early days claimed the sovereignty of the narrow seas that washed her coasts, and required foreign vessels meeting an English man-of-war to dip their colors and to lower their sails as a salute. In the year 1200 a formal ordinance was issued instructing English ships of war to exact this homage. In 1554 a Spanish fleet was bringing Philip II, King of Spain, to England for his marriage with Mary, Queen of England. It fell in with an English squadron, and as the salute was not promptly given, the English admiral fired on the Spaniards, who then struck their colors and lowered their topsails.

Perpetual difficulties arose between the Dutch, the French, and the English in the narrow seas on account of these salutes;

---

* Ancient = ensign. It was probably the cross of St. George, as the Mayflower was an English vessel.

and in 1654 a treaty between England and Holland expressly provided that all Dutch vessels should acknowledge the English sovereignty by striking the flag and lowering the topsails. A treaty with France in 1673 provided that the war vessels of both nations should dispense with salutes.

England stoutly upheld her claim to be mistress of the narrow seas for more than five hundred years. At the present time all vessels on the seas (more than a marine league from the shore) are on an absolute equality. Vessels visiting a foreign port salute the foreign flag first by firing a prescribed number of guns; and their salute is promptly returned, gun for gun. All doubtful cases are settled by sending a junior officer to make arrangements beforehand, and difficulties never arise. There is a strict code of naval etiquette that is entirely familiar to all concerned.

Surrender is signified by hoisting a white flag, or by hoisting the flag of the conqueror above the flag of the conquered. A flag hoisted at half mast with the union *downward* is a sign of distress, or of some accident. A yellow flag signifies that there is sickness on board. It is allowable to hoist "false colors"—a flag not your own—on a ship, to deceive an enemy in time of war.

A merchant ship, for example, chased by an enemy, would be justified in hoisting the flag of a neutral nation to make the pursuer abandon the chase. A man-of-war might hoist her enemy's flag to entice the foreign ship within gunshot, etc. But it would not be considered honorable to hoist a signal of distress and to bring the hostile ship near on an errand of mercy, in order, afterward, to destroy her. There is a line of distinction in such matters that is observed among all civilized nations.

THE FLAGS OF FRANCE.

Flags came into general use in Europe about the seventh century. They were often religious in their origin. The *oriflamme* of Charlemagne (A. D. 800) was given him by the pope, who at the same time commemorated the foundation of the new empire of the West by striking a medal with the motto, *Renovatio Imperii.**

---

* The Roman Empire was divided into the Eastern and the Western Empires in A. D. 364, and it came to its end when Rome was captured, in A. D. 476, by Odoacer, King of the

The cords to Charlemagne's banner were red and white and blue, and these afterward became the colors of France by a mere coincidence.

The blue hood or cape of St. Martin, a religious banner, was used by Clovis, King of the Franks, about A. D. 428. St. Martin was a soldier as well as a saint, and his banner was a truly warlike one. The oriflamme of Charlemagne was the banner of the emperor rather than the standard of the empire.

The famous oriflamme of St. Denis was originally merely the banner of an abbey; but it afterward took its place in the armies of the French

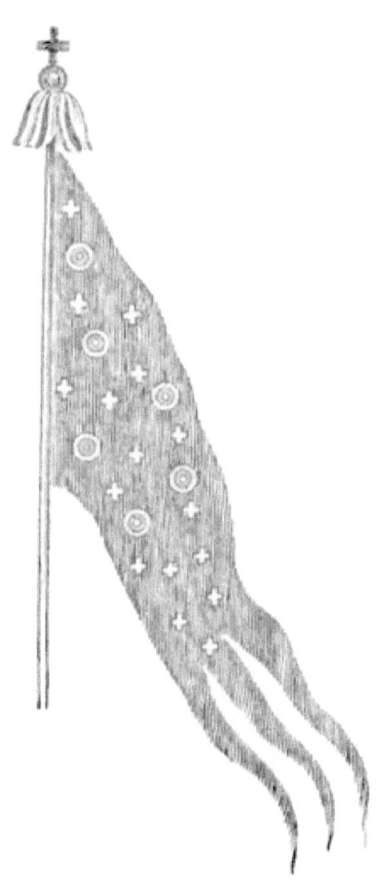

Fig. 45.—The oriflamme of Charlemagne, A. D. 800.

Heruli. Charlemagne founded a new empire called "of the West," and the medal celebrates the "renewal of the empire."

king, and became a truly national symbol. A national flag must be uniform, universal, obligatory. It must represent the beliefs of the nation and its unity.

The oriflamme was in the first place—about A.D. 630—a sacred banner to be carried in processions by the monks of the Abbey of St. Denis, near Paris; and miraculous powers were attributed to it. The Counts of Vexin were the hereditary knights-banneret of this abbey, and so long as they held this office, and the abbey lands that pertained to it, the ban-

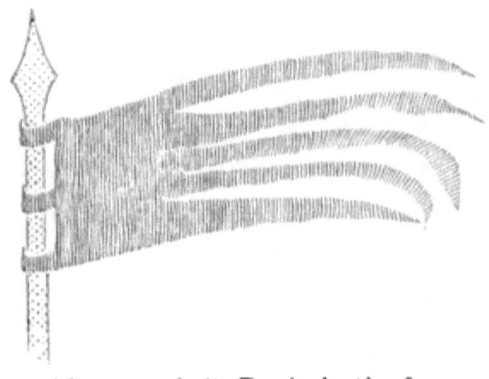

FIG. 46.—The oriflamme of St. Denis in the form employed in the thirteenth century. In later times there were only two points to the pennon-tail.

ner had a local meaning only. But about A.D. 1100 the King of France held this office and the lands, and the banner became, in this way, his banner, and in some fashion the banner of France also. It stood for religion, too, and its reputation for working miracles was a great help to the king.

It was first displayed by a king of France in 1124, and often afterward. The kings went in great state to the abbey when the banner was brought out. It was confided to the care of one of the bravest knights, who swore "to carry that standard to the honor and profit of the king and of his realm; never to lay it down for fear of death or of any hazard; and to do his duty everywhere." This brave oath was lived up to by a succession of the stoutest knights of France.

The miraculous power of the oriflamme was fully believed in by the soldiery. In the war with Flanders, in 1382, it is recorded that "all the morning there had been so great and so dense a fog that scarcely could the men see one another. But so soon as the knight that carried the oriflamme proceeded to unfurl it and to raise the staff aloft, this fog all at once fell and dispersed—the sky becoming pure and clear." Others said that a white dove then appeared and sat on the king's banner for a good omen.

It was supposed by the soldiers that an

army could not be defeated while it carried the oriflamme, but the troops of St. Louis of France (Louis IX) were defeated in the seventh Crusade by the Saracens, the king was made captive, and the oriflamme fell into infidel hands (A. D. 1250).

Like most of the flags carried by the Crusaders the oriflamme terminated in three points, to mark the fact that the French were fighting for the doctrine of the Trinity against the Saracens, whose war cry was "there is no other god but Allah." In earlier times such flags usually terminated in five points, and the number of points was then without any special meaning.

After the Crusades pointed flags were usually of the pennon form; they terminated either in a single point or in two points—a swallow-tail, so called. In a general way, it is safe to refer a flag of three points to the period of the Crusades; its three points were a symbol of the Trinity.

The oriflamme continued to be used as a national flag throughout the thirteenth and fourteenth centuries. It was taken from the abbey by the king in state for the last time in 1415. In the fifteenth century, during the wars with the English, it became a red ensign with a white cross. In later years the oriflamme gradually lost its national character, and the royal standard took its place. It was the king's standard that was advanced by the Maid of Orleans (1429 - '31); although she also carried a white banner with religious emblems.

Since the time of Louis VII the arms of France have been *fleurs-de-lis* (flowers-de-luce, the iris) borne on a field of blue. In 1179 his coat of arms was a blue shield sprinkled with many fleurs-de-lis. Charles V. in 1364, reduced their number to three; and three fleurs-de-lis on an azure field has been since then the royal shield of France. No one knows the reason for the adoption of the fleur-de-lis as the emblem of the French kings. The emblem itself is very old, and it has been displayed in many

FIG. 47.—The arms of France— golden lilies on a blue field.

places. The Empress Theodora of Constantinople (A. D. 527) wore one in her crown.

The emblem of the city of Florence is a fleur-de-lis that was originally white. After a bloody battle (A. D. 1251) its color was changed to red, in memory of the brave Florentines who perished, it is said.

From the thirteenth century onward till the reign of Louis XIV the blue flag with fleurs-de-lis was more and more used as a national ensign. White was the color of the Huguenot party in France with Henry IV at their head, but the royal standard was blue as before. Louis XIV (acceded 1643) was an absolute ruler and extremely jealous of his own authority. The high officers of his army were called colonels-general, and the troops under their command were the soldiers of the colonel-general quite as much as they were the soldiers of the king. Each colonel-general bore a white flag as a sign of his pre-eminence.

The king determined to be master of his own army, and he assumed for himself the office of colonel-general of all the troops, and took the white flag charged with the royal coat of arms in the center as his personal standard. "The white flag of the Bourbons" has no more ancient origin than this. It represents, as no other flag does, the supreme authority of a king.

The colonels of regiments at this time had tricolored flags—red, white, and blue. And red, white, and blue were the personal colors of King Henry IV of France (died 1610). Red and blue were the colors of the city of Paris, and white was the royal color. In 1794 the French revolutionary convention formally adopted the tricolored flag as the national standard, as the flag of the French people. It has three vertical bars of equal width. The bar nearest the staff is blue, the center bar is white, the fly is red. The tricolor of France is shown in Plate V.

In 1792 the revolted people of Paris took a red flag as their symbol. By a strange, unconscious choice the red flag has since become the standard of all revolt, the flag of any angry and violent protest. It is not the flag of a particular cause, but it has covered all kinds of revolts, excusable and inexcusable, against all kinds of constituted authority, just and unjust.

It has represented the assassinations by the Nihilists in Russia and the bloody massacres by the anarchists in France, as well as the peaceful protests of labor against the oppression of employers. It has stood for causes with which every generous heart must sympathize, as well as for revolts that every good citizen must abhor and condemn.

A flag that has served as the standard of the murderers who shot the innocent hostages in Paris in 1871 discredits, so far as a flag can, movements and aspirations otherwise worthy of respect and sympathy.

The red flag is unique among symbols. It is the only banner known to history that stands for no cause in particular and that symbolizes no positive creed, belief, or hope. It is the banner of destructive overthrow of things as they are at the moment, not the symbol of a desire to reconstitute things as they ought to be in the future. Even the black flag of piracy stands for a positive desire.

If we compare the meaning of the red flag with that of the ensign of revolted New England (Fig. 8) we shall comprehend this difference. The flag of the colonists stood for their union to secure, by force if necessary, certain specific liberties that were the birthright of all Englishmen. It represented positive beliefs and hopes, and a union for the purpose of maintaining them.

The red flag represents anarchy—overthrow, revolt—as its only ideal, and a transitory union of forces for the purpose of attaining chaos. Until the essential character of the red flag is changed, it is the duty of every law-abiding citizen to oppose all causes that shelter themselves under this symbol. If a cause is just, let it choose its own symbol and let it be judged on its own merits. The most righteous cause can not afford to appear under colors like these.

When Napoleon I became emperor, in 1804, the tricolor remained the flag of the nation. The armies of France had won such amazing victories under this standard during the years since 1789 that it was endeared not only to the soldiers but to the people. Every Frenchman was proud of it. Napoleon, who was skillful in directing public and private feeling into channels that were favorable to his own fortunes, did not fail to use the flag to strengthen his influence.

The colors of every regiment in the army were inscribed "The Emperor to the ——

Regiment," and the soldiers were thus continually reminded that their very flag was a gift from their chief. Their fortunes depended on his favor. The regimental standards were borne on staffs with the imperial eagle at the head. Napoleon dreamed of a new empire of the West not less extended than that of Charlemagne, and he chose his symbols so as to inspire the imagination of his subjects.

On each flag he inscribed the names of the battles in which it had been victorious. No soldier could see his battle flag without a proud thought of the victories of Lodi, Montebello, Arcola, Marengo, Austerlitz, and a hundred others. The Legion of Honor was instituted, and its cross was bestowed on Frenchmen who had served their country well.

Whenever a regiment had captured colors from the enemy in battle the cross of the Legion of Honor was awarded to the regiment, and it was suspended from the staff of the standard. Not every French soldier could win the cross of the Legion of Honor for himself, but he could at least help to win it for his regiment. A like custom prevails in other armies.

Russian regiments that have captured the colors of an enemy under fire receive the cross of St. George as a decoration for their flag. Prussian regimental colors are decorated with the iron cross, and also with the ribbons of the various war medals. The standards of the regiments of the German army are decorated with a ribbon of the German colors (red, white, and black) fitted with clasps of gold engraved with the names of battles in which the regiment has fought. The same custom prevails in the armies of Italy and Austria.

In England and in the United States the names of battles are inscribed upon the regimental flags. England gives the Victoria cross to individuals "for conspicuous bravery," and the Congress of the United States awards the medal of honor "for gallantry in action." It would be well to accord these distinctions to regiments and to ships as well as to individuals.

The imperial standard chosen by Napoleon was blue. It bore a golden eagle for the empire, and the field was sprinkled with golden bees Napoleon's personal emblem. The emblems of the ancient monarchy of

France were forgotten during the momentous years from the revolution (1789) to the battle of Waterloo (1815). The coats of arms of the new nobility created by Napoleon did not bear crosses and scallop shells (the symbols of the Crusades), but emblems derived from his own wars—pyramids, swords, etc.

At the restoration of the monarchy in 1815 King Louis XVIII took the white flag of the Bourbons with the royal arms (*azure*, three fleurs-de-lis *or*) in the center. The eagle at the head of the staff was replaced by the fleur-de-lis. The tricolor was abolished, but not forgotten. The monarchy had no victories to show like those that had been gained under the nation's flag.

In 1830 Charles X, the brother of Louis XVIII, was overthrown by a new revolution, and the new king—Louis Philippe—restored the tricolor in 1831. The new king called himself "the King of the French People." He was no longer the King of France "by divine right." The white flag of the Bourbons represented the theory that the king ruled by divine right. The tricolor represented the modern theory that he ruled by the will of the people.*

At the head of the flagstaff Louis Philippe set the Gallic cock for an emblem of France. This emblem was one of the caprices of Louis XIV. The cock was the emblem of the Gothic or of the Gallic legionaries of Rome (see Fig. 19) it is true, but it had no really continuous historic meaning, and it did not long remain. The coat of arms of 1830 bore the words *Liberty and order*.

In 1848 a French republic was proclaimed after a new revolution. The tricolor continued to be the flag of France, but the words *Liberté, egalité, fraternité* (liberty, equality, brotherhood) were inscribed on the center bar of white, as well as the word *Unité* (unity). The first three words represented the social idea of the time.

In 1851 Napoleon III (the nephew of Napoleon I) became " Emperor of the French." The tricolor was inscribed with the words *Honneur et patrie* (honor and our country),

---

* This is a theory that the world owes to the English. One of their famous moralists has bluntly said, "There is no more a divine right for kings than for constables," implying that the consent of the governed is the only warrant for power of any sort.

and the imperial eagle reappeared at the head of the standard and on the imperial coat of arms.

In 1871, after the disastrous war with Germany, the red flag of the Commune strove with the tricolor for pre-eminence in France. The tricolor won, as it deserved to win, and the French Republic to-day flies its historic flag of three colors, which stands for a century of struggle and for a hundred victories. The coat of arms of republican France is blue, and it bears the golden *fasces*—a battle-axe whose handle is composed of many separate rods bound together with scarlet bands. This was an ancient symbol of officers of the Roman Republic.

The tricolor is, no doubt, firmly established as the flag of the French people. It has not been without its perils, however, even in late times. In 1878 affairs in France were in confusion. There is little doubt that the Count of Chambord (grandson of Charles X) could have taken his place upon the throne as King Henry V if he had been willing to accept the tricolor as his flag—that is, if he had been willing to rule as a king chosen by the French people, and not as a king by divine right of succession from other Bourbon kings, his ancestors.

It was comprehended by every Frenchman in 1878 that the tricolor stood for one theory of government, and the majority of Frenchmen were determined to have a government of this sort. It was equally well understood that the white flag of the Bourbons represented a theory of government that France had rejected, once for all, in 1789.

The real issue was between two theories of government: Shall the French people be governed in this way, or in this other way? The question discussed was not a question of real issues, but a matter of symbols. Under which of two flags shall the king reign, if so be we have a king? The heir to the throne made a choice of a symbol—of a flag—and instantly the matter in hand was settled. The French people would not accept the chosen symbol.

The history of the flags of France affords a most striking example of the power of symbols. It shows that a symbol has a life of its own and a character; that it has something like a personality and may represent the cause or the aspiration of a people in much the same way that a chosen leader might do.

The oriflamme of St. Denis stood for the age of simple faith. The soldiery unquestioningly followed this religious banner to many victories. At the time of the Crusades the matter in men's minds was the struggle of the Christians to possess the sacred city of Jerusalem and the holy sepulcher of our Lord. In these times a cross was added to the plain red surface of the oriflamme. The cross went forth to subdue the crescent. The symbol of Christ was at war with the symbol of Mohammed.

The oriflamme was borne alongside the personal banner of the king, and it added force to his power. As years went on the real force of the kingdom was more and more concentrated in the king. All men saw that if the kingdom were to endure the king must be powerful. The Maid of Orleans— Joan of Arc—though most religious, advanced the king's banner and not the oriflamme.

Louis XIV gathered the whole power of France into his own hands. The white flag of the Bourbons was a symbol that the semi-independence of the provinces of France had been replaced by an authority centered in the person of the king.

The wild outburst of the revolution of 1789 overturned forever the ancient theory that the monarchs of France ruled by divine right. It threw the doors wide open for the admission of new ideas. The French nation—the solidarity of the French people—was born then, and the tricolor was its symbol.

The idea of nationality took a firm hold of the imaginations of Frenchmen at that time, and it has never been lost. They have held fast to its symbol—the tricolor—with equal tenacity. The inscriptions on the flag—*Liberty, equality, brotherhood*, or *Honor and our country*—have not endured simply because they were not adequate to symbolize the permanent aspirations and ideals of the people. The tricolor has persisted because it represents the feeling of all Frenchmen. If a full history of these symbols were to be written, it would be a history of France, or rather of the aspirations and beliefs of Frenchmen.

CHAPTER V.

THE FLAGS OF FOREIGN NATIONS—THE FLAGS OF SOVEREIGN STATES.

(The different countries are arranged alphabetically for convenient reference.)

THE present chapter contains a brief description of the flags of most of the sovereign states of the world, and of a few flags that belong to states not sovereign. Most of these flags are shown in Plates I to X in their true colors.

If there is any discrepancy between the plates and this chapter, the text is to be preferred to the plates.

Andorra.—The little state of Andorra has a flag divided by a vertical line into two halves. The half nearest the staff is gold, the other red. This flag floats over a state one hundred and seventy-five square miles in area and a population of six thousand persons. The colors are those of the old Counts of Foix, protectors of the state.

Abyssinia.—The coat of arms of Abyssinia is a lion bearing a cross and wearing a crown surmounted by a cross. Its flag probably bears this symbol.

Annam.—Annam has a flag of its own. It is a black flag nearly covered by a large yellow figure like an oblong diamond with flashing points. The kingdom is a protectorate of France.

Algiers.—Algiers has been a French colony since 1830. Its flag has seven horizontal stripes, white (uppermost), blue, red, white, red, blue, and white. (See Plate V.)

Arabia.—Arabia is now under Turkish rule. Its flag is shown in Plate X. The flag of Mohammed (and of the Fatimite caliphs) was green. The first flag was the green turban of the prophet, and was unfurled in A. D. 626. The green flag was preserved in Cairo till A. D. 1215, and is now in Constantinople, together with other relics. When a "holy war" against unbelievers in Mohammedanism is declared this banner is displayed to the "true believers." The Abbaside caliphs of Bagdad (A. D. 750–1258) used a black flag. The Ommiade caliphs in Arabia (661–750) and in Spain (755–1031) had a white banner.

Argentine Republic.—Its flag is composed of three horizontal stripes—blue, white, and blue, and the middle stripe bears a sun nearer the staff than the drawing in Plate IX. The merchant flag omits the sun.

Australia.—The flag of Australia is the flag of St. George (white, with a red cross) and the canton is blue, and bears a red cross, bordered white, and four white stars. It is the same as the flag of New Zealand, shown in Plate III. See BRITISH COLONIES.

Austria-Hungary.—See Plate VI. The flag of Austria is red, white, and red, arranged in three horizontal stripes. These are the ancient colors of Austria and of the Hapsburgs. The flag of Hungary is a tricolor of horizontal stripes, red (uppermost), white, and green. The war flag of the Austro-Hungarian monarchy is red, white, and red, with the Austrian coat of arms on the middle stripe. The flag of the merchant ships of the kingdom has its top stripe red, its middle stripe white, and its bottom stripe red for half the length, green for the rest, and the white stripe bears the coat of arms of Hungary as well as that of Austria.

The coat of arms of Hungary is not well shown in Plate VI. It is somewhat plainer in Plate X. Every province of the empire, as Bohemia (two horizontal stripes, the uppermost white, the lower one red); Moravia (two horizontal stripes, yellow and red); Silesia (two horizontal stripes, black and yellow); Dalmatia (two horizontal stripes, yellow and blue); Bosnia (three horizontal stripes, red, blue, and white); Croatia (three horizontal stripes, blue, white, and red), etc., has its own flag. The multitude of minor states that make up the dual monarchy have separate flags also.

Some of these flags stand for a history centuries long. The red and white of Austria is certainly as old as the fourteenth century. The flag of the Holy Roman Empire was yellow with a black eagle. The eagle was single-headed till the fourteenth century, when it was changed to a double-headed eagle. The arms of the Greek emperors of Constantinople in the thirteenth century contained a double-headed eagle, and the returning Crusaders brought this symbol with them. The symbol itself is far older, and goes back, in Asia Minor, to centuries before the Christian era.

Baden.—See GERMANY. Its colors, gold and red, were adopted early in the thirteenth century.

Bavaria.—See GERMANY.

Belgium.—See Plate VIII. The colors of the ancient Duchy of Brabant were black, yellow, and red. In 1831, on the foundation of the present kingdom, the tricolor flag of Belgium was established. At sea, at a distance, it has a strong resemblance to the ensign of France. The plate shows the royal standard. The merchant flag is the same, omitting the coat of arms.

Bohemia.—See AUSTRIA-HUNGARY. The ancient arms of Bohemia were a silver lion on a red field, and these colors are perpetuated in the flag.

Bolivia.—See Plate IX. The flag is divided into three horizontal stripes, red (uppermost), gold, and green. The center of the war flag bears the coat of arms.

Bosnia.—See AUSTRIA-HUNGARY.

Brazil.—The field of the flag of Brazil is green. On the field is a yellow diamond, which formerly bore the royal coat of arms of Brazil. The flag was copied from the flag of Portugal in the Indies (see PORTUGAL in what follows). The Brazilian Republic has replaced the royal coat of arms by a constellation of golden stars in a blue field, and a motto *Ordem e progresso*—order and progress—is now displayed (see Plate IX).

Bulgaria.—The flag of Bulgaria is a tricolor of three horizontal stripes, white (uppermost), green, and red. It was established in 1879 to replace the Russian flag that had formerly been in use. The war flag bears on a red canton the crowned golden lion of the national coat of arms. The colors are the same as those of Hungary, but their changed order commemorates the freedom of Bulgaria from foreign control (see Plate VIII). The merchant flag of Bulgaria is plain red.

Burmah.—Its white flag bears a red circle at the center, and the red circle is charged with a peacock.

Canada.—See Plate III. The red ensign of Great Britain is charged with the Canadian coat of arms. See GREAT BRITAIN, COLONIES OF.

Cape of Good Hope.—See GREAT BRITAIN, COLONIES OF.

Chile.—The ensign of Chile is divided horizontally into two stripes, white and red, and on the upper stripe is a blue canton bearing a single white star. The national standard bears, in addition, the Chilean coat of arms (see two pictures in Plate IX).

China.—See two pictures in Plate IX. The imperial standard of China (formally established in 1872) is triangular in shape and yellow. It bears a blue dragon and a red ball. Yellow is the imperial color in China, and the dragon is the emblem of the emperor. This flag in shape and in design has been displayed in China for centuries. It is very likely as ancient as the city of Babylon. The merchant flag is blue, bordered with red.

Cochin-China.—See Plate V.

Colombia (Republic of).—See Plate IV. The upper half of the flag is gold. The other half is divided horizontally into two stripes, blue and red. On the center of the flag is a red circle inclosing nine silver stars, one for each of the departments.

Costa Rica.—The flag has five horizontal stripes. The center stripe is red and is wider than the others. It is bordered by two white stripes, and the outer stripes are both blue. The war flag bears the national coat of arms (see Plate IV).

Congo Free State.—Its flag is blue and bears in the center a single golden star (Plate X).

Corea.—See Plate IX. Its white flag bears an ancient symbol in blue and red. This symbol is the *Pa-Kwa* diagram of China, and represents the system of opposites that runs through all Nature—earth and sky, water and earth, male and female, etc.

Croatia.—See AUSTRIA-HUNGARY. The colors are adopted from the ancient coat of arms of Croatia. Red, white, and blue are the national colors of the Slavs.

Cuba.—The flag of "Cuba libre" is composed of five horizontal stripes, alternate blue and white. At the head of the flag is a red half diamond bearing a silver star (see Plate II). The flag of the revolutionary party in Porto Rico (1898) is of the same design, but red takes the place of blue in the Cuban flag, and blue of red.

Dalmatia.—See AUSTRIA-HUNGARY. Blue and gold, the colors of the flag, are taken from the national coat of arms—three leopards' heads of gold on a blue shield.

Denmark.—See Plate VIII, two pictures. The raven was the emblem of the Danes in early times, and one of the banners of the Bayeux tapestry is supposed to represent it. In the year 1219 the Danes were Christians and were engaged in war with the heathen tribes of Prussia. In one of their battles the fortunes of the day were against them until a sacred banner—the Danebrog, the flag of the Danes—miraculously appeared among them. Under this banner, a white cross on a red field, they conquered, and since that time this symbol has been the flag of Denmark. Their king, Waldemar, instituted at that time an order of knighthood—the order of the Danebrog—which, under changed conditions, still exists.

The flag of Denmark is by far the most ancient of existing European flags. The cross of St. George has been in use as the English ensign since 1327, and the lilies of France were adopted on the coat of arms of the French kings in 1179. The green banner of Mohammed (A. D. 626) is still preserved at Constantinople. The royal flag of Denmark, and that of Sweden and Norway also, terminates in two points like a pennon. Most other modern ensigns are rectangular. The standard of Denmark bears the royal coat of arms. The merchant flag omits it.

Ecuador.—See Plate IV. Its flag is divided horizontally into two halves. The upper half is gold. The lower half is again divided into two stripes, blue (uppermost) and red. The flag of Ecuador was formerly white with a vertical central band of blue, on which were seven silver stars.

Egypt.—See Plate X. The flag of Egypt is red, and in its center it bears a silver crescent whose horns meet and nearly touch a silver star. This flag is the same as that of Turkey. The personal standard of the Khedive of Egypt has three crescents and three stars on a red field.

England.—See Chapter IV. The modern flags of Great Britain are shown in Plate III. The flag of England is St. George's cross without the union.

France.—See Chapter IV. The flag of France is shown in Plate V.

French Cochin-China.—See Plate V.

Geneva Red Cross Association.—A convention was held in Geneva in 1863 for the purpose of forming an international association for the succor of the wounded in time of warfare. In this and subsequent international congresses a society—the Red Cross Society—was founded, and it is recognized officially by nearly all civilized nations, and has done endless good in the alleviation of suffering. It has a flag—a red Greek cross on a white field—that is everywhere honored and respected. The Swiss flag (Plate X) with its colors interchanged—red for white and white for red—is the flag of the Association.

Germany.—See Plate VI. The flag of Germany (1871) is admirably composed to represent the colors of the chief kingdoms united in the empire. The German flag is composed of three horizontal stripes of black, white, and red. The flag of Prussia is two such stripes, black and white; Bavaria's is two stripes, blue and white; Saxony's is two stripes, white and green; Würtemberg's is two stripes, black and red;

Baden's is two stripes, red and gold. At least half of the flag of each of these ancient kingdoms is represented in the ensign of the empire, and several of them are there in their entirety. The flags of several of the smaller duchies—Hesse, Waldeck, Lübeck, etc.—are equally well represented in the combined flag. The imperial standard is shown in Plate VI. It bears the iron cross (the symbol of an order of knighthood), the black eagle (ditto) and four imperial crowns.* The red eagle of Brandenburg displays on its breast the black eagle of Prussia. The flag of the ancient German Empire from the end of the Middle Ages till 1806 was a black eagle on a golden field. This banner was certainly used as early as 1336, and probably much earlier. Black and gold were the German colors as early as A. D. 1214. The man-of-war flag is also shown in Plate VI.

Great Britain.—See Chapter IV and Plate III. The royal standard displays the quartered arms of Great Britain and Ireland. The proper flag of England is the cross of St. George without the union. The plate shows the banners of Scotland and of Ireland.

Great Britain, Colonies of.—Most of the colonies of Great Britain have badges or coats of arms. The revenue cutters and other vessels belonging to these colonies fly the *blue ensign* of Great Britain with the addition of the proper colonial badge in the middle of the "fly" of the ensign—that is, in the center of the space between the union and the tail of the

---

* Crowns of Charlemagne.

flag. These badges are circular disks of various colors, with a device of some sort upon the disks. Some of the badges are as follows·

CANADA.—The Dominion coat of arms. See Plate III for the badge.

CAPE OF GOOD HOPE.—The coat of arms of the colony, and the name of the colony Latinized, *Spes Bona*.

NEWFOUNDLAND.—A white disk, bearing a royal crown, and the name of the colony Latinized, *Terra Nova*.

NEW ZEALAND—A Greek cross of silver stars on a blue disk.

NEW SOUTH WALES.—A red cross of St. George with a silver star on each arm of the cross, and a lion at its center.

QUEENSLAND.—A blue Maltese cross on a white disk, with a crown at the center of the cross.

SOUTH AUSTRALIA.—A landscape of rocks and sea, the goddess Britannia and a native Australian.

VICTORIA.—The southern cross on a blue shield, surmounted by a royal crown, all on a white disk.

WEST AUSTRALIA.—On a yellow disk a black swan.

These are the flags to be flown by the vessels of the colonial services, and are presumably the official flags of the colonies. Canada has been granted an official flag, which is the red ensign of England, with the badge as above (Plate III).

Greece.—See Plate VIII. The merchant flag of modern Greece has nine horizontal stripes of blue and white, and a blue union charged with a white Greek cross. It dates no further back than 1832, when Otho I, Prince of Bavaria, became King of Greece, and brought the blue and white colors of his family with him. It would seem that some symbols of the ancient glories of a country with so extended a history might have been adopted in its standard. The royal standard ensigns the cross with a golden crown.

Guatemala.—Its flag is of three vertical bars, blue, white, and blue. See Plate IV.

Hawaiian Islands.—See Plate II. The present flag of the Hawaiian Islands has eight horizontal stripes. The upper stripe is white, then red, blue, white, red, blue, white, and red. The blue union bears St. George's and St. Andrew's crosses in red with white borders.

The history of the flag of the Hawaiian Islands (now a part of the territory of the United States) is briefly as follows: In 1793 the explorer Vancouver gave an English flag to the king to be used as his colors, and a traveler reports that the British flag was flying over the king's residence in 1808. In 1816 the flag of the islands was described as "the English Union Jack with *seven* alternated red, white, and blue stripes." An English naval officer in 1825 declares that it consisted of "*seven* white and red stripes, with the Union Jack in the corner." The present flag has *eight* stripes, one for each of the islands—Hawaii, Maui, Kahoolawe, Lanai, Molokai, Oahu, Nihau, Kanai. The latter island was under an independent king until 1821, and it is probable that its stripe was not added until 1845, for the *Polynesian* newspaper of May 31, 1845, says: "At the opening of the Legislative Council, May 25, 1845, the new national banner was unfurled, differing little, however, from the former." It is fully described in that publication, and agrees exactly with the present flag. The first, fourth, and seventh stripes are silver; the second, fifth, and eighth are red; the third and sixth are blue. Since the Hawaiian Islands were annexed to the United States in 1898 their national ensign is, of course, the American flag. Their old colors will probably be flown as a State or Territorial flag.

Hayti.—The merchant flag of Hayti is divided horizontally into two halves—blue (uppermost) and red. See Plate IV. The war flag adds the national coat of arms on a white square at the center of the flag.

Holland.—See NETHERLANDS.

Honduras.—Its flag has three horizontal stripes, blue, white, and blue, and the central stripe bears five azure stars. See Plate IV.

Hungary.—See AUSTRIA-HUNGARY.

Iceland.—It is a colony of Denmark and flies the Danish ensign.

Italy.—See Plate VII. In early times each city of Italy had its own banner. Milan about the year 1035 displayed its banner from the top of a mast set in a chariot drawn by white oxen. The fashion was copied by other cities and passed into England soon afterward, as we have seen. The chariot (*carriocium* in Latin, *carroccio* in Italian) was guarded by stout warriors and was set in the midst of the troops. So long as it maintained its place the battle was going well. When it was captured or overturned the day was lost.

The Florentine emblem is the lily. The legend recites that the army of Florence was sore pressed in a battle with the barbarians in A. D. 405, when St. Reparata suddenly appeared bearing a red banner with a white lily for device and turned the fortunes of the day. The lily of Florence was white until A. D. 1251, when it was changed to red in memory of the blood of her citizens that had been shed in the conflicts between the parties of the Guelphs and of the Ghibellines.

The present flag of Italy is a tricolor of three vertical stripes of green (next the staff), white, and red. It was established in 1861. White and red are the colors of the reigning royal house of Savoy, and green was added as the color of hope—hope for a United Italy. The tricolor of green, white, and red was adopted by the provisional government of Venice during the revolution of 1848, and the same colors were given to the kingdom of Italy by Napoleon I. The war flag (see Plate VII) bears the arms of the house of Savoy on the center bar. The royal standard bears the same arms on a white field bordered blue. The Savoy arms are those of the Sovereign Order of St. John of Jerusalem, and were granted to the Duke of Savoy in 1309 as a mark of gratitude for his help in the defense of the island of Rhodes against the Saracens.

Ireland.—See Chapter IV and Plate III.

Japan.—See Plate IX. For something over twenty-five hundred years Japan has been a military nation. Six hundred and sixty years before Christ the present reigning family came to the throne; and the emperor is the one hundred and twenty-second of his line.* If we go back to 660 B. C. in the history of our Western world, it takes us to the time of Nebuchadnezzar, King of Babylon, whose story is told in the Old Testament. There is no dynasty in Europe that compares in age with this. The Bourbons of France date from A. D. 884 only; the Hapsburgs of Austria from 952.

The history of Japan is in many respects like that of Europe in the Middle Ages. The system of government was in both cases the feudal system. The nominal head of Japan was the emperor (the *Mikado*). From very early times the real power was usurped by a military chief—the *Shogun*—who ruled in the name of the Mikado. The first shogun dates from the fourteenth century. One powerful family —the Tokagawas—held the shogunate from 1602 till 1868. In the latter year they were overthrown, and the Mikado is the head of modern Japan, as he was of the Japan of ancient days. The various provinces were governed by the *daimios* (like earls and counts in Europe), and each *daimio* maintained a court in his capital city. The great lords of Japan had learned men and artists in their train as well as soldiers, and courtesy and chivalry were practiced everywhere.

The Japanese warriors were as fierce and warlike as the Crusaders or as the feudal barons of the Middle

---

* Failing a direct male heir to the throne the family is recruited by the adoption of a nephew or of a cousin of the emperor.

Fig. 48.—Ancient standards of Japan, with weapons and musical instruments.

Ages in Europe. But our own ancestors chose for their emblems beasts of prey, like the lion and tiger, fierce birds like the eagle, fabulous animals like the dragon or the wyvern. The Japanese, on the other hand, with their gentle and cultivated feeling for art and manners, almost always selected beautiful, simple, even humble emblems—flowers, birds, butterflies, geometrical patterns. The dragon was a symbol of the emperor's power in Japan, but it was not taken as the principal emblem of the imperial family. Instead of this, the chrysanthemum, a beautiful flower, was chosen.

The Crusaders thought it necessary to emphasize their own courage and strength by choosing emblems among the savage beasts. The Japanese warrior of the same period felt that his courage and bravery would be taken for granted, and he wished his symbols to recall beautiful and artistic forms and courteous high-bred manners. A curious example of this characteristic difference survives to this day in the Japanese custom of releasing a flight of white doves when a war ship is launched. The European habit is to break a bottle of wine over the prow of the ship.

The national flag is shown in Plate IX.

The white field of the Japanese flag carries a red circle—" the circle of the sun "—and this emblem was in use by the emperor at least as early as A. D. 1169, though it was not formally adopted as a national flag until 1859. The flags of Japan and of China are the oldest of national flags. The flag of Denmark—by far the oldest in Europe—was not adopted until 1219.

The first mention of flags in Japanese history is in connection with the invasion of Corea by her army in A. D. 201. The Japanese standard that foreign countries are most likely to see is the standard displayed on her ships of war. It is the flag of her armies as well. Its field is white, and the red circle of the sun is the center of a series of red diverging rays that suggest the leaves of the chrysanthemum—the imperial badge.

Liberia.—The flag of Liberia is of the same design as that of the United States. It has six red stripes and five white ones. Its blue canton bears a single silver star. (See Plate IX.)

Luxemburg.—The flag of Luxemburg is a tricolor of three horizontal stripes, red (uppermost), white, and blue.

Madagascar.—While Madagascar was a protectorate of France it had a flag, as shown in Plate V, and presumably this is still its flag as a French colony.

Malta.—The flag of Malta (which is now a British possession) is shown in Plate III. See THE SOVEREIGN ORDER OF ST. JOHN OF JERUSALEM in this chapter.

Mexico.—The tricolor of Mexico has three vertical bars, green (next the staff), white, and red. The eagle seizing a snake and the cactus in the Mexican coat of arms is an ancient Aztec symbol. (See Plate IX.) The merchant flag is the tricolor without this coat of arms. The principal banner of the army of the *conquistadores* of Mexico under Cortez (1519) was of black velvet bearing a red cross. A religious banner of the expedition is still preserved at the city of Mexico. It is of red damask, and bears on one side a picture of the Virgin Mary, on the other the quartered arms of Castile and Leon (see Fig. 1). One of the banners of Pizarro borne by his army in the conquest of Peru was preserved in Lima until the present century, but it was lost in one of the many revolutions of the country.

Monaco.—Its flag is composed of two horizontal stripes, red (uppermost) and white. The territory of the principality is three miles by one and a half miles, and the flag floats over twelve thousand five hundred and forty-eight inhabitants.

Montenegro.—The flag of Montenegro is the same as that of Servia, namely, a tricolor of three horizontal stripes, red (uppermost), blue, and white. See Plate X. Montenegro has another ensign of three horizontal stripes (red, white, and red), bearing a white cross in the upper and inner corner, which is the flag of its merchant ships. The colors red and white are derived from the coat of arms of the family of Palæologus, Greek emperors of Constantinople in the thirteenth, fourteenth, and fifteenth centuries. The arms of the Palæologi were a white double-headed eagle on a red field, and these are the arms of Montenegro. The arms of the reigning prince are a golden lion on a green mound in an azure field. The flag sometimes bears one of these coats, sometimes the other. The illustration in Plate X shows the cipher of the prince beneath a crown.

Moravia.—See AUSTRIA-HUNGARY. Its colors—gold and red—were adopted in 1848, during the revolutionary period, and they repeat the tinctures of the eagle on its ancient coat of arms.

Morocco.—The flag of Morocco is red, with the device of two crossed scimitars shown in Plate VIII. The merchant flag is plain red.

Netherlands.—(Two pictures, see Plate VIII.) The national flag of the Netherlands has three horizontal stripes of red (uppermost), white, and blue. For centuries Holland had no separate existence. It was a part of the Duchy of Burgundy from 1436 to 1477, then a province of Austria, passing to Spain in 1506. The independence of the Dutch Republic was not recognized until 1648. The colors of the house of Orange (orange, white, and blue) served as the national standard through long and troublous years, until the orange gradually changed, without any special reason for the change—about 1660—into red, and since that time there has been no change.

Newfoundland.—See GREAT BRITAIN, COLONIES OF.

New South Wales.—Its flag has a white field with a blue cross charged with five silver stars, and its canton bears the union jack of England. See also GREAT BRITAIN, COLONIES OF.

New Zealand.—See Plate III. See also GREAT BRITAIN, COLONIES OF.

Nicaragua.—The maritime flag of Nicaragua has five horizontal stripes, blue, white, red (in the center), white, and blue. See Plate IV.

Norway.—See SWEDEN. See also Plate VIII.

Orange Free State.—Its flag has seven horizontal stripes, four white and three orange. A canton (of the width of the uppermost three stripes) is divided into three horizontal stripes, red, white, and blue (the lowest) in order. See Plate X.

(The Sovereign) Order of St. John of Jerusalem.—The order of knighthood called St. John of Jerusalem (Knights of Rhodes, 1310-1522, and after 1522 Knights of Malta) was founded in the year 1048 to be of service to the Crusaders. The order grew rich and very powerful, and it took a flag just as a nation might take a standard. Its flag is red with a white cross, and is at least as old as 1130. As the order still exists its flag has a place in this book. The order is called "sovereign" just as France is called a sovereign state; and in Europe its flag is saluted and respected just as is the flag of France. It is never seen in America. The *standard* of the order is black, and bears a silver Maltese cross. There were other orders of knighthood of the same kind (the Knights Templars, etc.), but they are now abolished. This one still lives. Any good encyclopædia gives some account of such orders under the heading of KNIGHTHOOD.

Papal State.—The flag of what remains of the Papal State is composed of two horizontal bars, the uppermost gold, the lower white.

Paraguay.—See Plate IX. Its tricolor flag is divided into three horizontal stripes, red (uppermost), white, and blue. The center stripe is the widest, and it bears the national coat of arms.

Persia.—See Plate X. The white flag of Persia is bordered with green, and it bears the device of the kingdom, namely, the lion and the sun in yellow.

Another Persian ensign is a tricolor of horizontal stripes, green (uppermost), gold, and white.

Peru.—See Plate IX. The modern flag of Peru is red, white, and red, in three vertical bars. The war flag bears also the national coat of arms. In the army of the Incas each company had its banner, and the standard of the emperor was emblazoned with the rainbow—the emblem of the "children of the sun."

Philippines.—The flag of the insurgents in the Philippines, 1898, is divided into two halves by a

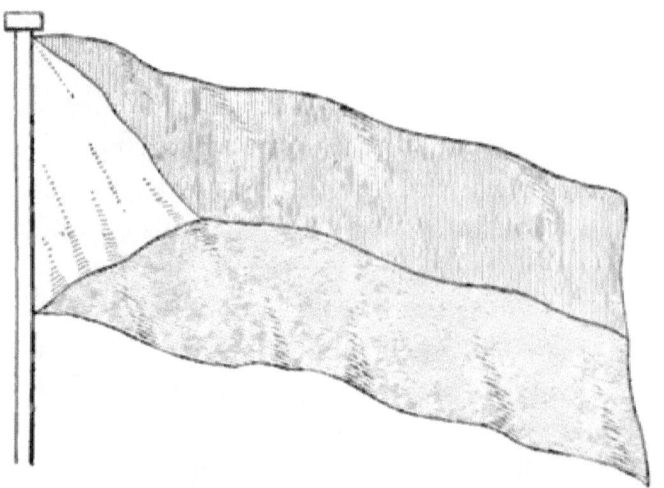

Fig. 49.—The flag of the Insurgent Philippines, 1898.

horizontal line. The upper half is red, the lower blue. Next the staff is half of a white diamond.

Poland.—The ancient coat of arms of the kingdom of Poland was a white eagle on a red field, and white and red are the national colors. They were adopted by the revolutionists of 1846. The kingdom is divided and has no separate flag.

Portugal.—See three pictures in Plate VIII. The merchant flag of Portugal is half blue and half white, with the line of division vertical, and the royal coat of arms is placed at the center of the field of the *ensign*. It was adopted in 1815, but it is a modification of the ensigns of the earlier centuries when Portugal was a great commercial power, and when her hardy navigators opened Africa and the Indies to Europe. The flag of Portugal in the Indies bore an armillary sphere (an instrument used by navigators), and this device was displaced in the ensign of Brazil so long as it was an empire. The royal standard of Portugal is red, and displays the king's arms.

Prussia.—See GERMANY.

Puerto Rico had no separate flag, but flew the flag of Spain. The flag of the insurgents in Puerto Rico (1898) is composed of five horizontal stripes of red and white. At the head of the flag is a blue diamond bearing a single silver star. The design of the flag is the same as that of Cuba, with the colors interchanged.

Queensland.—See GREAT BRITAIN, COLONIES OF.

Roumania.—See Plate X. The flag of Roumania is a tricolor of vertical bars—blue nearest the staff, then gold, then red. These colors were adopted during the revolutionary times of 1848.

Russia.—See Plate VII. The national flag of Russia is a tricolor of horizontal stripes, black (uppermost), orange, and white. This is not shown in the plate. The war flag is white, with a blue St. Andrew's cross. The flag of merchant ships is a tricolor of horizontal stripes, white (uppermost), blue, and red. The imperial standard is orange colored, with the double-headed eagle of the empire bearing on his breast the national coat of arms, viz., a silver St. George and the dragon on a red shield.

Samoa.—Its flag has a white field with a black cross. On a red canton there is a silver star.

San Marino.—The little republic of San Marino has a flag of seven horizontal stripes, alternate blue and white. The republic dates from the fourth century. It has eight thousand inhabitants.

San Salvador.—The flag is like that of the United States in design. It has five blue stripes and four white ones. Its union is red and bears nine silver stars. See Plate IV.

Santo Domingo.—The Dominican Republic. See Plate IV. Its merchant flag bears a white cross, and the angles of the cross are filled as follows:

blue	red
red	blue

The national ensign adds a coat of arms at the center of the cross.

Sarawak.—It has a yellow flag on which a cross is displayed. The half of the cross next to the staff is black, and the other half is red.

Saxony.—See GERMANY. The ancient colors of Saxony were black and gold, and since A. D. 1151 a green wreath has been borne on its coat of arms. The Saxon kings of Poland took the Polish colors, red and white. Black and gold were the colors of Saxony until the end of the Napoleonic wars of 1813-15. On the restoration of the king in 1815 white and green were established as the Saxon colors.

Scotland.—See Chapter IV and Plate III.

Servia.—The flag of Servia is a tricolor of three horizontal stripes, red (uppermost), blue, and white. The flag of Montenegro is the same design. The royal standard bears the coat of arms. See Plate X.

Siam.—The red flag of Siam bears in its center a white elephant. See Plate V.

Silesia.—See AUSTRIA-HUNGARY. The colors—gold and black—are derived from its ancient coat of arms—viz., a black eagle on a gold field.

Society Islands.—See Plate IX.

South Australia.—See GREAT BRITAIN, COLONIES OF.

Spain.—The Spanish flags are shown in Plate VIII. Many changes have been made in the standard of Spain, which has usually borne the royal coat of arms. The castle of Castile, the lion of Leon (see Fig. 1), the pomegranate of Grenada, the lion of Flanders, the red, white, and red of Austria, the *palle* (pills) of the Medicis, the eagle of the Tyrol, the *fleurs-de-lis* of France, the gold and azure diagonal bars of ancient Burgundy, the red and gold bars of Aragon, and the arms of Sicily—all these emblems appear in the royal shield.* The merchant flag of Spain is a yellow field with two narrow red bars, and is probably derived from the arms of Aragon, though the colors are also those of the shield of Castile.

Sweden and Norway.—See Plate VIII. The national flag of Sweden is blue, and bears a golden cross; the national flag of Norway is red, and bears a blue

---

* Which is not accurately drawn in Plate VIII.

cross with a white border. These flags and crosses have been united in modern times (Norway was joined to Sweden in 1814) to form one flag, somewhat in the fashion of the union flag of England. The man-of-war flags of both countries have pennon tails (like the royal standard of Denmark, shown in Plate VIII).

Switzerland.—See Plate X. The Swiss flag is red, and it bears a Greek cross of white in its center. The Switzers declared their independence in 1307, and at the battle of Morgarten (1315), where the Austrians were defeated, they carried a plain red flag without any device. During the seventeenth century a white cross was added, though it is said that the cross appeared on some Swiss flags as early as 1339. The different cantons of Switzerland have different coats of arms and different flags.

Tahiti.—Its flag has three horizontal stripes of red, white, and red, and on a canton the French tricolor of vertical bars, blue, white, and red. See the last figure in Plate IX.

Tonga Islands.—The flag is red; on a white canton it bears a red Greek cross.

Transvaal (South African Republic).—Its flag has three horizontal stripes, blue (uppermost), white, and red. Next the staff is a vertical band of green. The drawing in Plate III shows an earlier flag, now superseded.

Tripoli.—See Plate V. Its flag is red.

Tunis.—The war flag of Tunis is red. It bears a white oval at its center and a red crescent and star are superposed on the oval. See Plate V. The merchant flag is plain red.

Turkey.—See two pictures in Plate X. The present war flag of Turkey is red, bearing near the staff a silver crescent encircling a silver star. The Turks also carry a standard divided horizontally into two bars—one red, the other green. The merchant flag of Turkey is pictured in the last figure of Plate X. The crescent was the emblem of Diana, patroness of Byzantium, and it was used on many Christian banners before the Turks assumed this emblem for their own. From that time forward the crescent became an exclusively Moslem symbol, as opposed to the cross, the symbol of the Crusaders.

United States of America.—See Part I of this book, Chapters I, II, and Plates 1 (frontispiece) and II.

United States of Venezuela.—The flag has three horizontal stripes, gold (uppermost), blue, and red. At the center is a cluster of seven silver stars, one for each State. See Plate IV.

Uruguay.—Its flag has nine horizontal stripes, alternate white (uppermost) and blue. On a white canton is a golden sun. See Plate IX.

Victoria.—See GREAT BRITAIN, COLONIES OF.

West Australia.—See GREAT BRITAIN, COLONIES OF.

Würtemberg.—See GERMANY. The colors of Würtemberg are black and red. Its ancient coat of arms contained three *red* lions. When the heir to the throne of Naples (Conradin of Suabia) was defeated and beheaded, in 1268, the lions were changed to *black*, and these colors are still represented in the flag.

Zanzibar has one flag shaped like a pennon, with a swallow tail. All the stripes are horizontal. The top stripe is narrow and is red. The next stripe is narrow and white. The next is narrow and green. Then comes a wide white stripe, with three green crescents. The next stripe is red, and the next green, and these two stripes are wider than the narrowest ones and not so wide as the widest one. The middle stripe of the flag is wide, and has three green crescents. Then come red, green, wide white (with three green crescents), narrow red, narrow white, narrow green stripes in order. A plain red flag is also flown. See Plate III.

(3)

THE END.

www.ingramcontent.com/pod-product-compliance
Lightning Source LLC
Chambersburg PA
CBHW020242170426
43202CB00008B/186